The Dragon of Wantley

A pantomime

Norman Robbins

Samuel French — London
www.samuelfrench-london.co.uk

Please see page iv for further copyright information

CHARACTERS

Mauxalinda, a vengeful fairy
Sir Walter de Warthog, Mayor of Wantley
Rags ⎫
Tatters ⎭ Sir Walter's bailiffs
Squire Benjamin Moore
Granny "Verruca" Gubbins, housekeeper to the Squire
Lady Joan, Sir Walter's ward
Madge Merry, Lady Joan's lady-in-waiting
Vendetta, Mauxalinda's servant
Jingo, Squire Benjamin's valet
Radish, the Squire's horse
Mother Shipton, the famous Knaresborough Witch
The Dragon (optional)
Chorus of **Villagers**, **Servants, Dancers** and **Children**

SYNOPSIS OF SCENES

ACT I

ACT II

COPYRIGHT MUSIC

MUSICAL NUMBERS

ACT I

1	Song	(*Villagers*)
2	Song	(*Squire*)
3	Song/Dance	(*Jingo and/or Villagers*)
4	Song	(*Squire and/or Villagers*)
5	Song	(*Madge*)
6	Song	(*Lady Joan and Villagers*)
7	Song	(*Rags and Tatters*)
8	Song	(*Squire and Joan*)
9	Song/Dance	(*Villagers*)
10	Song	(*Squire*)

ACT II

11	Song/Dance	(*Villagers*)
12	Song	(*Granny, Rags and Tatters*)
13	Song	(*Squire*)
14	Dance	(*Maids and Footmen*)
15	Song/Ghost Gag	(*Sir Walter*)
16	Dance	(*Creatures*)
17	Song	(*Joan*)
18	Song	(*Full Company*)
19	Song	(*Jingo and Audience*)
20	Music	(*Walk Down/Reprise*)

DESCRIPTION OF CHARACTERS

Mauxalinda, a vengeful fairy whose figure should appear gaunt, swathed in dark shades of silken material

Sir Walter de Warthog, the pompous Mayor of Wantley, dressed in his official robe, hat and chain

Rags and **Tatters**, his bailiffs, are an ill-matched pair, one has clothes too large and the other too small. Scruffy brown tabards are worn over dingy, patched, ballet shirts and dark knee breeches, grubby white or yellow stockings, floppy soft hats and buckled shoes. Wigs in pudding-bowl styles would also look good. For the wallpaper business they wear quick-washable trousers and shirts. Tatters' shirt is of the rip-away type with a velcro-ed front panel, and both wear their usual hats.

Squire Benjamin Moore, the impoverished Squire of Moore Hall, is a handsome young man in balloon sleeved shirt, a tunic and tights but changes into an all silver costume (shirt, tunic, tights, shoes, cloak gauntlets, etc.), to kill the dragon at the end of Act I

Granny "Verruca" Gubbins, is a lady of uncertain age, housekeeper to Squire Benjamin, and desperate for romance. She wears a series of outrageous frocks

Lady Joan, is the ward of Sir Walter, and wears a full length medieval gown complete with a conical head-dress and silk chiffon plumes trailing down her back

Vendetta, Mauxalinda's servant, is a brutal-looking man, dressed in a black tunic over a dark green pirate shirt with a belt, black tights and soft shoes. Needs to be strong enough to carry Lady Joan over his shoulder

Jingo, Squire Benjamin's valet is a zany character, not too bright, but usually cheerful. In Act II he wears a garish but quick washable outfit, which should be similar to his usual style of costume

Radish, the Squire's horse

Mother Shipton, the famous Knaresborough Witch, is very old, almost bent double, with a hooked nose and long upturned chin. Though dressed as a traditional witch, she is kindly and gentle

Madge Merry, Lady Joan's buxom lady-in-waiting, is middle-aged, loyal and easy going, but not the brightest button in the box. She wears a simpler version of her mistress' costume

The Dragon, optional

Chorus of **Villagers**, etc.

AUTHOR'S NOTE

The Dragon of Wantley is another of those huge, spectacular pantomimes so beloved by Victorian audiences, yet in the 21st century is totally forgotten by all but historians. It took its first bow at the Covent Garden Theatre, (now the Royal Opera House) as a burlesque opera on October 26th, 1737 and ran for 67 performances in its first season, (five more than *The Beggars Opera*, nine years earlier). Written by Henry Carey, composer of the ballad *Sally in our Alley*, and great grandfather of the famous actor, Edmund Kean, with music by John Frederick Lampe, it was directed by John Rich, the inventor of British pantomime. It continued to delight audiences for many years, but in 1870, the great pantomime writer E L Blanchard decided the storyline could appeal to the working classes if the "highbrow" element was removed, and transformed it into a spectacular pantomime for the Theatre Royal, Drury Lane. With scenery by the legendary William Beverley, and featuring not only the infamous Volkes Family, but a 150 strong company, it was one of his greatest successes. Modern audiences, however, would have found much to mystify them had I simply updated Blanchard's masterpiece. Pantomime in Victorian times was a far different animal and its humour stemmed from very different sources. In writing my version of this story (based on an English legend involving real people), I have discarded the great spectacular scenes that were used merely to dazzle and amaze, and concentrated on the comedy. Some of the character names are those used by Cary and Blanchard, but the rest are my own invention. I hope you'll have as much fun performing this unusual subject as I had writing it.

Norman Robbins

PRODUCTION NOTES

There is little in this script to cause anxiety for prospective pantomime producers, but perhaps a word or two on the dragon would be appreciated. Knowing the difficulty of obtaining specialised costumes at "panto time" (someone else always has the Giant, or Cow, etc.) I have written it in a way that the Dragon is never actually seen, though if you can obtain a costume, it can be dropped into the script with no problem whatsoever. There are also various ways to use the dragon. Halls with only limited space need only have the head appearing from the cave. Larger halls can accommodate the whole dragon, having several people inside it to give it mobility. It can be a Welsh dragon, (costumiers who can supply costumes for "Merrie England", would have this kind in stock), or an ornamental Chinese dragon could fit the bill. Many years ago, we made a fabulous dragon's head from polystyrene blocks cut to shape and painted, for a local carnival. The smoke effect described in the script, is provided by a smoke machine which can be hired fairly cheaply from good Lighting and Special Effects Companies. The sound of the dragon is played through an offstage speaker, and almost any animal roar or bellow will suffice. If the dragon is used in the pantomime, it should enter as Squire backs out of the cave so the fight takes place onstage. If it is not used, follow the stage instructions. For the "Slosh" scene, I suggest that a waterproof cloth be set on stage before the scene begins. The other cloths help soak up the mess. For ADS.'s, cans of cheap shaving foam are possibly the best solution for the wallpaper paste, but a substitute can be made with flour and water, or very thin wallpaper paste with colour added. Make sure there are plenty of cloths handy for mopping up the actors. If the wallpaper is tightly rolled, the lengths will roll up again quite easily. It is also essential that the stepladder is held tightly by another character during its use. The quick change for the Mayor in the Dragon scene is done by under-dressing the damaged shirt and trousers, and him clutching his Mayoral Robe about him to conceal these as he enters. Once off-stage, he replaces the good robe with the ragged and scorched one and lets it hang loose. There would also be time for him to apply sooty marks to his face before re-entering.

N.R

For

Paul Taylor

With thanks for his support and encouragement over
the past thirty-five years

"The old magician's final flourish."

PROLOGUE

The main CURTAINS *open to reveal a gloomy grotto tucked inside the gnarled roots of an ancient tree. Mauxalinda stands glowering* C, *bathed in red and green light*

Mauxalinda (*balefully*) Behold the home of Mauxalinda,
               Greatest of the forest fays.
               Here I dwell in damp and dark,
               And have done so for all my days.
               Beneath the earth I've lived content
               Quite undisturbed by man...
               But now my peace is shattered by
               Some stupid, local council plan.
               The land above, (*indicating*) which once they claimed
               Had great outstanding beauty,
               They've sold to some developer,
               In dereliction of their duty.
               (*Angrily*) Now instead of grassy fields,
               And trees, so tall and great,
               They'll cover it with offices —
               Or some industrial estate.
               (*Seething*) But by my troth, though "progress"
               Is the image they dissemble —
               Upon their heads I'll place a curse
               To make those idiots tremble.
               From hence, the lands of Wantley
               Shall be wracked with fear and dread
               And all who live inside its bounds
               Will very soon be dead.

She gives a spiteful and triumphant laugh and exits L

The Lights go out

ACT I

Scene 1

Wantley Village Square

A typical medieval pantomime village setting with thatched cottages set against a back-drop of thickly wooded hills. Exits L *and* R *are masked by shops or houses*

It is a bright and sunny day and the Villagers are dancing and singing

Song 1

At the end of the song, Sir Walter de Warthog enters UL *and moves down centre, rudely pushing his way through the Villagers*

Sir Walter (*grandly*) Stand aside, peasants. Make way for your Lord and Master.

Villagers move back reluctantly

Old Villager (*scowling*) You baint our Lord and Master, Walter de Warthog. You baint nothing but a mean, bad tempered old so-and-so with too much money. Our real Lord and Master is young Squire Benjamin of Moore Hall.

Villagers agree

Sir Walter (*sneering*) Yes, but not for much longer. Unless he pays the Council Tax he owes, by this time next week he'll be homeless. (*He smirks*)

Villagers react in dismay

Villager Two (*protesting*) But you know he can't pay his Council Tax. All the money he had was used to pay off his late father's debts. He's sold everything he owned—including the furniture—to put things right again.

Villagers agree

Sir Walter (*sneering*) How very upsetting. But don't expect me to show any sympathy. I offered to buy his house and land as soon as his father died, but he refused to sell.

Villager Three (*scornfully*) I'm not surprised. His family have lived there for hundreds of years, and he wouldn't want a crook like you to get his hands on their property.

Villagers agree

Sir Walter (*outraged*) How dare you cast nasturtiums on my character? I've half a mind...

Villager Four (*perkily*) Well at least you admit it.

Villagers laugh and exit variously

Sir Walter (*scowling; annoyed*) Bah. They'll be laughing on the other side of their faces, before very long. (*Smirking*) Little does Squire Benjamin know it, but the writing desk I bought from him last month had a secret drawer, and inside I found the title deeds to Moore Hall and all its fantastic grounds. (*Gleefully*) With those in my hands, I've made an absolute fortune by selling everything to developers without a soul knowing about it. By the time they find out, Moore Hall will be gone for ever, and the whole area will be covered in warehouses, wind farms, and rows of second-rate superstores. (*Laughing*) Then as soon as it's finished, I'll be off in my private yacht leaving everybody else to put up with the noise and inconvenience. (*He chortles with delight*)

Rags and Tatters enter upstage

Rags (*spotting Sir Walter*) Ooooh. (*Grabbing Tatters' arm*) Quick. Quick.

They rush down to Sir Walter, positioning themselves one at each side of him

(*Cheerfully*) Mornin', Sir Walter. (*Beaming at him*)

Sir Walter (*to the audience*) Bah. It's those idiot bailiffs of mine, Rags and Tatters. I've been searching for them all morning. (*To Rags; Grimly*) Where've you been?

Tatters Looking for the burglar who broke into the health food shop last night and pinched all the prunes and figs.

Sir Walter (*scowling*) And did you find him?
Rags No. He's still on the run.

Sir Walter reacts

But on the way here, we saw six drunken yobbos beating up (*a well known politician*).
Sir Walter And did you rush to help?
Tatters No. We thought six could do the job easily.
Sir Walter Bah. You're the stupidest bailiffs I've ever had. You haven't a brain between you.
Rags (*indignantly*) Oh, yes we have. (*Proudly*) When I was at school, I got straight "A"s.
Sir Walter (*surprised*) Really?
Tatters Yes. But all his other letters were wobbly. (*He chortles*)
Sir Walter (*scowling*) Well now you are here, you can make yourselves useful. According to my information, there's a well known witch called Mother Shipton heading this way, making prophecies and telling fortunes. I want her arrested the minute she gets here for not having a licence.
Rags (*doubtfully*) Ooooh, I don't know about that, Sir Walter. It doesn't pay to upset witches. One of 'em put a terrible curse on my Uncle Fred and he's not been the same since.
Sir Walter Really?
Rags Yes. She gave him three wishes.
Sir Walter (*scowling*) Three wishes? What's terrible about that?
Rags Well, he was a bit daft to start with. So first of all he wished to be ten times brainier and suddenly, he was. So he got himself a job as a shop assistant in Tesco's and earned hundreds of pounds a year. Then after a while, he got fed up and wished he was fifty times brainier. Two weeks later he was working in a bank earning thousands of pounds a year. Then finally he wished he was a hundred times brainier.
Sir Walter And what happened?
Rags He turned into a woman.

Rags and Tatters chortle

Sir Walter (*annoyed*) Bah. Enough of this drivel. Find Mother Shipton at once, and lock her in the stocks till I return from the dentist.

He exits DR

Tatters (*watching him go*) Ooooh, I hope he's not going to the one I went to last week. I only called in to ask a question and he was real nasty to me.

Rags Why? What did you want to know?

Tatters Well my teeth were a bit on the yellow side, so I asked if he could recommend something.

Rags And what did he say?

Tatters "Try wearing a brown *tie*."

Rags (*wincing*) Well never mind about that. What are we going to do about this witch?

Tatters We'd better make a plan. I'll tell you what. We'll go down to (*local café or restaurant*) and get something to eat while we're thinking.

Rags No fear. I'm not going in that place again. The manager doesn't like me.

Tatters (*curiously*) How do you know that?

Rags Because the last time I went in there, I ordered egg, chips and peas, and when he brought it over, there were no peas on the plate.

Tatters That doesn't mean he doesn't like you. He'd probably just forgotten them. You should have reminded him.

Rags (*protesting*) I did. I did. And he said "You're one of Sir Walter's new bailiffs, aren't you?" And when I said "yes", he said "Well in that case, you must be as big a crook as he is—and everybody knows there's no peas for the wicked."

Tatters snatches his hat off and beats Rags around the shoulders with it

(*Howling*) Oww. Oww. Owww.

They exit DR *still fighting*

Squire Benjamin enters UL *and moves* DC *glancing around sadly as he does so*

Squire Benjamin (*sighing*) Well, it looks like it's goodbye to Wantley unless I find money from somewhere. I haven't a penny left in the world. (*Cheering up*) Still... At least I've paid everyone's wages, so there's only myself to worry about. For the first time in my life, I can leave the village and explore the world on my own two feet. (*Thoughtfully*) I wonder what's out there? (*To the audience*) I've heard of the Pyramids, and I'd love to see those. And London's a wonderful place— according to my late father—but there must be millions of interesting places I've never been to. I can't wait to see them all for myself. (*Dreamily*) Disney World... The Grand Canyon... The City of

New York. (*Happily*) Who cares that I'm penniless if I can face everyone with a smile on my face and a song in my heart?

Song 2

At the end of the song, he exits DR *, and as he does so*

Granny Gubbins enters UL *and moves* DC

Granny Gubbins (*to the audience*) Ooooh, I say... Look at the crowd tonight. (*Chuckling*) Can't be much on television. (*Peering at them*) I see Mrs Jones is in again... (*She waggles her fingers at her*) Did you find him, love? ... No? Oh, I am sorry. (*Explaining to the rest of the audience*) Her little Chihuahua ran off last week and she couldn't find him anywhere. "Put an ad in the (*local newspaper*)," I told her "You might get a reply." "Oh, I don't think so," she said, "He never learned to read." (*Spotting someone else*) Oh, and there's Mr Brown from the garage. (*To him*) We were at school together, weren't we? (*To the audience*) Oh, yes. I remember his dad giving him a real telling off for coming home one day with a settee and two armchairs some feller had given him. (*Pausing*) Well, he had been warned not to take suites from strangers. (*Chuckling*) Oh, but here's me going on about people in the audience, and you don't even know who I am, do you? Gubbins is the name. Verruca Gubbins. Housekeeper to the Squire of Moore Hall (*coyly*)...and widow of this parish. (*She curtsies and beams*) Funny old name, isn't it? Verruca. But don't worry, it'll grow on you. (*Seriously*) Mind you... I've been working at Moore Hall for so long, everybody calls me Granny. (*Incredulously*) Granny? Me. (*Primly*) I don't look a bit like a Granny, do I? There might be some snow on the mantelpiece, but the fire's still burning I can tell you. (*Seriously*) Mind you... I don't know why I'm telling you all this. According to the council's accountant, we've got to move out of the Hall tomorrow. (*Scornfully*) Council's accountant. They haven't invented calculators yet, so he has to do all his sums on his fingers and toes. Yes. The only way he can count up to twenty-one is to take his clothes off. (*Brightening*) Still... if I have to find another job, I can always go back to nursing. (*Beaming*) No. Don't look so surprised. I used to work at (*local hospital*) till I got this job. If it hadn't been for me, Gordon Brown (*or another politician*) might never have been cured. They brought him in with a terrible cough and nobody could help him. Poor fella could hardly stand upright. "Leave it to me," I said and gave him a glassful of stuff from the medical cupboard. He swallowed it in one gulp, stood absolutely upright, walked outside and leaned against his Rolls Royce. "What on earth have you given him?" said the specialist, "None of us could do anything." "Well," I said, "I gave him half a pint of Syrup of Figs." "Syrup of Figs," he said, "But that's for constipation. It won't stop his cough." "Yes, it will," I said, "Look at him now. He's too scared to cough."

Lady Joan enters UR

Seeing Granny Gubbins, she hurries DS *to her*

Lady Joan (*breathlessly*) Granny Gubbins.
Granny Gubbins (*to the audience*) Oooh, I say—it's Lady Joan, Sir Walter's ward. (*She turns to her and curtsies*)
Lady Joan (*anxiously*) It's not true, is it? You're not really leaving Moore Hall?
Granny Gubbins (*shrugging*) We haven't much choice. That rotten guardian of yours is throwing Squire Benjamin out. In a few more days he'll be off to seek his fortune, and the rest of us'll be out of work...
Lady Joan (*dismayed*) But he can't leave Wantley. I may never see him again.
Granny Gubbins (*surprised*) Why should you care? This time next week you'll be married to Sir Walter.
Lady Joan (*puzzled*) What?
Granny Gubbins Well, that's what he told Squire Benjamin. You were going to be married as soon as he'd made the arrangements.
Lady Joan (*indignantly*) But it's not true. I wouldn't marry Walter de Warthog if he was the last man on earth.
Granny Gubbins (*brightening*) You wouldn't? Oh, I am pleased to hear it. I'd hate you to be married to a man who knew so many naughty rude songs.
Lady Joan (*surprised*) I've never heard him singing naughty rude songs.
Granny Gubbins No. But he's always whistling them. (*Excitedly*) Still—never mind that. Just wait till I tell Squire Benjamin you're not getting married. He'll stay here forever.
Lady Joan (*fervently*) Oh, I do hope so. And if it's only money he's worried about, then as soon as I'm twenty-one, his worries will be over. My father left me a fortune, and I'll gladly give every penny of it to him.
Granny Gubbins (*wistfully*) Ooooh. I wish somebody would leave me a fortune. My late husband, Cyril, tried once, but it didn't do any good. (*Glancing round to see if anyone is listening*) He had an e-mail from his friend in Australia to say he'd been waiting at a bus stop for a bus to come along, and when one did, he stuck his leg out instead of his hand and the bus ran straight over it. (*Wincing*) But luckily, he'd just got insured against accidents, and got thousands of dollars in compensation. "Oooh," said my Cyril, "I could try that and get myself thousands of pounds." So he insured himself against accidents and went off down the road to wait for a (*local bus company*) bus.

Lady Joan And what happened?

Granny Gubbins He died of starvation.

Lady Joan (*amused*) Oh, you do make me laugh, Granny Gubbins. And I'm so glad you weren't thinking of leaving, too.

Granny Gubbins Oh, I couldn't leave this place? I've lived here all my life. (*Coyly*) Twenty-eight years. (*She simpers, then glowers at the audience reaction*)

Lady Joan (*interested*) So you'll remember what it was like before Sir Walter built Humbug Hall?

Granny Gubbins Oh, yes. When I was a girl, there was nothing but fields and forests all around us. And as for the weather, oooooh, it used to be terrible. Nothing but thick, thick fog for months and months on end. I was eight years old before I saw my Mum and Dad.

Lady Joan (*laughing*) Now I'm sure that's not true. But before you tell me any more fairy stories, I think we'd better find Squire Benjamin and tell him I won't be marrying my guardian, no matter what he claims.

Granny Gubbins (*beaming*) I can't wait to see his face.

They exit together UR

The Lights dim

Mauxalinda enters DL *in a green light*

Mauxalinda To Wantley, now, by my command,
A stranger comes from foreign land,
Who carries in his horse-drawn waggon,
Eggs of some stupendous dragon.
Here upon a bed of thatch,
To lie in secret till they hatch,
Then henceforth shall these mortal folk
On searing flames and sulphur choke. (*Glancing off* L)
But hark. The sound of slippered feet
Approaching down this cobbled street.
(*Smirking*) That furtive step can only mean
Vendetta's now upon the scene.

Vendetta enters UL

He has a dagger is in his belt and is carrying a small casket. On seeing Mauxalinda, he moves to her and kneels, displaying the casket. She looks at it, scowling, then glares at him

(*Venomously*) Speak quickly. Does this chest you bear
Contain those dragon eggs, so rare?

Vendetta (*fearfully*) Great Mistress. Forgive me. My horse was lame, and by the time I reached the dragon's lair, all eggs but one had hatched.

Mauxalinda (*angrily; indicating the casket*) And this?

Vendetta The smallest egg of all. (*Anxiously*) But even so, Great Mistress, still warm—and almost ready to hatch.

Mauxalinda (*raging*) You fool. You dolt. You idiot.
My orders were quite clear.
Your tardiness has spoiled my plan.
I swear 'twill cost you dear.

Vendetta cowers

(*Hesitating*) And yet—as ev'ryone must know
Great oaks from tiny acorns grow... (*She takes the casket from Vendetta and gazes at it*)
Perhaps this single egg so small
Shall hatch the fiercest beast of all?
With magic spells to aid its birth
In hours its cries could shake the earth.
And ere the rising of the sun,
Begin consuming everyone.
(*To Vendetta; coldly*) For now, my anger fades away.
I'll let you live another day.
But from henceforth, the servant of the Dragon you
shall be.
And Wantley and its councillors shall bow their heads
to me.

She swirls around and exits DL *with the casket*

Vendetta exits hurriedly after her

The green light fades, Lighting returns to previous setting

Jingo hurries on UL *looking worried*

Jingo (*calling anxiously*) Radish? (*Glancing round quickly*) Radish? (*Anguished*) Oooooh, where's he got to? (*Seeing the audience and hurrying down centre*) Here. You've not seen a horse called Radish, have you?

Audience respond

No? (*Groaning*) Ohhhhhh. He's Squire Benjamin's favourite horse and I'm supposed to be looking after him. He could be half-way to (*local town or village*) by this time. Ooooh, I am fed up. (*Relaxing*) Still... I don't know why I'm worrying. Once today's over, I won't have a job. I'll have nothing to do but wait for Dame Fortune to come knocking on my door. (*Ruefully*) Mind you—with my luck it'll probably be her daughter... Miss Fortune. (*Sighing then remembering*) Oh—but I haven't introduced myself, have I? You don't know who I am. (*Beaming*) Jingo's the name's. (*Spelling it*) J-I... (*hestitating*) ingo. Squire Benjamin's valet. Can you remember that?

Audience respond

Can you?

Audience respond

(*Doubtfully*) Ooooh, you don't sound too sure. So I'll tell you what we'll do. Every time I come on, I'll shout "Hi ya, kids" and you can shout back "Hi ya, Jingo" so I'll know you've not forgotten. Shall we do that?

Audience respond

Shall we?

Audience respond

All right. We'll have a little practice, then. (*Calling*) "Hi ya, kids"

Audience respond

Well—it's not bad, but I'm sure you can be louder than that. Let's try it again. (*Calling*) "Hi ya, kids"

Audience respond

That's better. Well now you know who I am. You can help me look for Radish, because we'll need him to pull the cart when we have to leave Moore Hall. So I'll look over here (*Indicating* DL) and you look over there (*Indicating* R) and if you see him...give me a shout. Will you do that?

Audience respond

Jingo moves L *to peer off*

   Radish gallops on UR *and butts Jingo, knocking him into the wings*

   There is a yell of surprise from Jingo followed by a loud clattering offstage. Radish moves C, *shaking with laughter*

   A moment later, Jingo reappears, his head inside a bucket or watering can

   Ooooooh. (*He pulls the bucket off and sees Radish*) You naughty, gee-gee. What did you want to do that for? (*He puts the bucket down and crosses to Radish*) And where've you been? I've been looking for you all over.

Radish whispers in his ear

   You've been watching your brother running in the Grand National?

Radish nods

   And did he win?

Radish shakes his head then whispers again

   What do you mean? He was too polite. How could he lose a race for being polite?

Radish whispers again

   Every time he came to a fence, he stopped and let the jockey go first.

Radish nods then whispers again

   But you think it should have been a photo finish?

Radish nods

   And didn't they have one?

Radish shakes his head, then whispers

   Oh, I see. By the time he got to the finishing line, it was too dark to take photos.

Radish nods

Well, never mind all that. Now you are here, would you like to say hallo to all the boys and girls in the audience?

Radish shakes his head

(*Surprised*) You wouldn't?

Radish whispers

You want to say hallo to the posh lady. (*Puzzled*) What posh lady? (*Peering into the audience*)

Radish nods in direction

(*Seeing her*) Oh... you mean her. (*Frowning*) What makes you think she's posh?

Radish whispers

She's picking her nose with a knife and fork. (*Outraged*) Radish. (*To their victim*) I'm terribly sorry, Missis. I do apologize. He was only joking. (*Hastily*) No, no. There's no need to put them away. Carry on digging. (*To Radish, sternly*) That was very naughty, Radish. And here's me just about to tell everybody how clever you are.

Radish hangs his head

She might have wanted to buy you.

Radish looks up in alarm

Well—we can't afford to keep you now we're being thrown out of the Hall. And there's lots of people looking for clever horses, you know. Just show the boys and girls how well you can add up. (*To the audience*) Watch this, kids. (*To Radish*) How many is two and two?

Radish paws the ground six times

(*To the audience*) You see? What did I tell you? Two and two make...
(*Realizing*) Just a minute. Just a minute. (*To Radish*) Two and two
don't make six.

Radish nods his head

Oh, no they don't.

Radish nods firmly

(*To audience*) Tell him, kids. (*Encouraging audience*) Oh! No, they
don't...

Audience respond

Radish nods firmly stamping his foot again six times

(*To Radish*) All right, then. All right. I'll prove you've got it wrong.
How many legs have you got?

Radish paws the ground six times

(*Annoyed*) No, you haven't.

Radish nods, then whispers to him

You've got two legs at the back, and forelegs in front.

Radish nods and laughs as Jingo rolls his eyes

(*Defeated*) All right. You've had your little joke. Now behave yourself
and give the boys and girls a nice curtsy.

Radish does a polite curtsy

Now what else can I tell them about you?

Radish whispers

(*Surprised*) You can dance better than Billy Elliot?

Radish nods

(*Scornfully*) I don't believe that. (*To audience*) Do you, kids?

Audience respond

(*To Radish*) You see? (*Scornfully*)What sort of dance can a horse do?

Radish whispers

A tap dance? Don't be daft. I've never seen you tap dancing.

Radish whispers

You had to stop because you kept falling into the sink (*Disgustedly*) Well I don't believe you can dance at all. In fact, unless I see it with my own eyes, I'm never going to believe it. All right?

Radish stiffens with indignation, then nods to the musical director who begins to play a lively tap dance which Radish skilfully performs

As he does so, the Villagers enter gradually L and R and look on with amazement

This can be worked up to a big production number if required, and lyrics sung by Jingo and/or the Villagers

Song/Dance 3

As the routine draws to a close, Radish exits DR, followed by Jingo who picks up the bucket, leaving the Villagers to end the song

As the audience applause dies down, Mother Shipton enters UR, leaning on a gnarled stick

Villager One (*alarmed*) A witch. A witch.

With cries of fear, all cower from her

Mother Shipton (*moving down centre*) A witch indeed, of great
                                renown,
                        Who comes from far off Knaresb'rough Town.
                        No need to fear me. Hear my claim.
                        Old Mother Shipton is my name.
Villager Two (*amazed*) Mother Shipton? The famous fortune-teller?

All relax and look excitedly at her

Mother Shipton   'Tis true. The future I can read,
                     So journeyed hence with all due speed.
                     To bring you warning, one and all—
                     Misfortune here will shortly fall

All react with dismay

                     Your Mayor, greedy, sly and proud.
                     Has breached the limits he's allowed
                     And so by doing—all unwary—
                     Roused a most indignant fairy.
                     Now her vengeance hurtles down
                     On unsuspecting Wantley Town.
Villager One   (*aghast*) You mean it's all Walter de Warthog's fault?

Everyone looks angry

Mother Shipton   (*regretfully*) Alas. It cannot be denied.
                     And all because of greed and pride.

Everyone reacts as Sir Walter enters DL, *followed by Rags and Tatters*

Sir Walter   (*seeing Mother Shipton*) It's the Witch I told you to arrest.
Grab her.

Rags and Tatters rush behind him and grab Mother Shipton as the Villagers jeer

Silence, you vociferous vulgarians. Or I'll have you all thrown into
jail. (*To Mother Shipton*) How dare you enter Wantley without my
permission? We'll have no witches here. (*Grandly*) To the ducking
stool with her.

Rags and Tatters try to drag Mother Shipton away

Squire Benjamin enters DR

Squire Benjamin   (*firmly*) Just a moment. What's going on?
Sir Walter   (*snapping*) You keep out of this, I'm in charge now.
Squire Benjamin   (*amused*) Oh, no, Sir Walter. Until I leave Moore
Hall, I'm still the Master of Wantley village. (*To Rags and Tatters*)

Release that lady, at once.

Rags and Tatters quickly release her

Now someone tell me what's happening.
Villager Two This is Mother Shipton, the famous Knaresborough witch.
(*Indicating Sir Walter*) And she came to warn us about him.
Sir Walter (*outraged*) Me? (*Blustering*) Don't be ridiculous. What have
I done?
Mother Shipton (*accusingly*) Beneath those ancient lands you've sold.
For untold bags of gleaming gold,
There lived a fairy, quite serene,
'Till contractors came on the scene.
Soon ev'ry tree they axe or saw
Will crash down to the forest floor,
And in their place, as she suspected,
Superstores will be erected.
Comet, Tesco, and so on...
With all wildlife forever gone.

Villagers look horrified

Sir Walter (*sneering*) So what? Who's bothered about a few flowers
and a bunch of creepy crawlies? What Wantley needs is affordable
housing.
Mother Shipton Then mark my words, Your doom is sealed.
This moment, o'er in yonder field, (*indicating* L)
Inside a scarecrow, ragg'd and patched,
A baby dragon's being hatched.

The Villagers look shocked

With fright'ning speed, 'twill grow and thrive
Till nothing here remains alive.
Squire Benjamin (*protesting*) But this has nothing to do with us. We
didn't know Sir Walter had sold any land.

The Villagers agree

Surely there's something we can do?
Mother Shipton (*shaking her head*) Unless, by chance, some valiant
knight
Shall challenge it in armour bright

And battle through the night and day—
In Wantley he'll forever stay.
For who round here can name a boy
Whose sword a dragon could destroy?

Everyone looks worried

Squire Benjamin (*bravely*) Well I don't know if I could kill a dragon—
but I'm certainly not going to stand by and let it do just what it wants.
(*To the Villagers*) If whoever bought my sword will lend it back to me,
I'll do my very best to put it to good use.

Everybody brightens

Mother Shipton (*kindly*) Well said, young Squire. But there's no way
Your sword, this monstrous beast could slay.
Protected by a fairy's power
'Twill grow more fearsome by the hour

All look worried

(*Thoughtfully*) And yet... Your courage might prevail
And all here live to tell the tale.
For as the ancient legends tell,
There are some ways to break a spell.

All look at her hopefully

(*Deciding*) Into the future I must gaze,
Discovering the means and ways
By which, despite its fiery blast,
That savage foe could breathe its last.

Squire Benjamin (*valiantly*) Then please do it quickly, for as long as
there's breath in my body, not even a dragon's going to take away this
village's happiness.

The Villagers cheer loudly. Sir Walter scowls

Music begins under the cheers

Mother Shipton exits R, unnoticed by the Villagers

Sir Walter exits DL in a temper, followed hastily by Rags and Tatters

As the cheering fades, Squire Benjamin sings

Song 4

If required, the Villagers can join in the second verse of the song As it ends in a semi-tableau, there is a rapid fade

SCENE 2

Down Kiss-Me-Quick Lane

Lady Joan enters R, *followed by Madge Merry*

Madge (*worried*) Oh, Lady Joan. I don't want to be eaten by a nasty old dragon.

Lady Joan (*patiently*) You won't be, Madge. I've already told you. It's only a small one and as soon as Mother Shipton tells him how to kill it, Squire Benjamin will polish it off long before it's a danger to anyone. (*Kindly*) Now why don't you go back to Humbug Hall and have a little rest? You look so tired.

Madge (*mournfully*) I am. I didn't get to bed till four o'clock this morning.

Lady Joan (*surprised*) Why not?

Madge Sir Walter told me to put his cat out for the night, so I had to stay up and wait for it coming in. (*She yawns*)

Lady Joan (*kindly*) Never mind, Madge. I'll take care of the cat tonight. You have a good night's sleep. You don't want to miss the fun at tomorrow's Goose Fayre.

Madge (*brightening*) You're right. (*Delightedly*) At last year's Fayre, a lovely young man kissed me so passionately, I could hardly breathe.

Lady Joan (*surprised*) Who was it?

Madge I don't know. I'd never seen him before.

Lady Joan (*puzzled*) Then how did it happen?

Madge Three other girls held him down for me. (*She giggles*)

Lady Joan (*amused*) Oh, Madge. You're the funniest lady-in-waiting I've ever had, but you really mustn't chase after every man who catches your eye. There's plenty good fish in the sea, you know.

Madge (*sighing*) Yes. But who wants to marry a fish? (*Gloomily*) It's all right for you, Lady Joan. Squire Benjamin's the handsomest man in the village. But there isn't a chance of somebody like me finding a husband.

Lady Joan Why not? There are dozens of single men in Wantley.

Madge (*downcast*) Yes. But none of them want to get married.

Lady Joan (*surprised*) How do you know?

Madge Because I've asked them all. (*Disgustedly*) And as for that feller in (*local shop or store*) the less said about him, the better.

Lady Joan Why? What happened?

Madge He said he'd ask me to marry him if I'd give him a kiss and a cuddle down (*local lover's lane*). So off we went, and after a few hours, I told him it was time he proposed.

Lady Joan And didn't he do it?

Madge No. He just laughed in my face and told me to jump in the pond.

Lady Joan (*dismayed*) Oh, no.

Madge Yes. And by the time I got back again, he'd gone. (*Plaintively*) Oh, if only I knew what was wrong with me? Why can't I catch a man and keep him.

Song 5

After the song, Lady Joan and Madge exit L

As they do so, Vendetta enters R, *scowling*

Vendetta So this is the village of Wantley? No wonder Mauxalinda wants it destroyed. Everywhere looks clean... There's no graffiti... and worst of all, the people are happy. It's absolutely revolting. (*Leering*) Still... it'll all change for the better once the dragon's big enough to eat anything. But in the meantime, a few children will make it a tasty snack. (*Menacingly*) I wonder if there's any around here. (*He moves* L, *peering into the audience*)

Granny Gubbins enters R, *in an amazing new creation and moves* C, *without noticing Vendetta*

Granny Gubbins (*excitedly; to the audience*) Oooh, I say, boys and girls. Fancy having a dragon in our little village.

Vendetta scowls at her

It's the most exciting thing that's happened in years. (*Correcting herself*) Well—except for the time that (*well known personality*) came here to give a talk on Chronic Fatigue Syndrome. (*Ruefully*) Mind you—it didn't work out. We were all too tired to go. (*Beaming*) But it's worrying, isn't it? Having a dragon on your doorstep. I mean we've all heard the stories, haven't we? How they like to eat pretty young girls for their breakfast. (*Worried*) I hope he doesn't come looking for me.

Vendetta (*scornfully*) You, you bilious-looking bag of bones. He wouldn't touch you with a barge-pole.

Granny Gubbins (*noticing Vendetta for the first time*) Oooh, I say it's Simon Cowell. (*Or another well known male with a caustic tongue*)

Vendetta (*moving towards Granny Gubbins*) For your information, Madam, I am Vendetta, servant of Mauxalinda the fairy, and guardian of the baby Dragon.

Granny Gubbins (*wide-eyed*) And is that your bottom lip, or are you wearing a polo-necked jumper?

Vendetta (*glowering*) Bah. For two pins, I'd break you into little pieces and scatter them to the winds.

Granny Gubbins (*unfazed*) You wouldn't have said that if my fourth husband was alive. (*Proudly*) He was the heavyweight boxing champion of Britain. (*To the audience*) We were walking down the street once, and a masked feller rushed up to him, stuck out his gun and said "Hand over your money or I'll shoot".

Vendetta (*sneering*) And what happened?

Granny Gubbins (*to Vendetta*) Nothing. He just gave him the five hundred pounds he had in his wallet...

Vendetta (*incredulously*) Without fighting for it?

Granny Gubbins (*patiently*) I've just told you. He was the heavyweight champion of Britain. He never fought for less than a million.

Vendetta (*disgusted*) Bah. Is everyone in this place as stupid as you are?

Granny Gubbins (*indignantly*) I beg your puddin'. Who are you calling stupid? I got an award last year for stopping cars speeding through the village at ninety miles an hour.

Vendetta (*sneering*) Really?

Granny Gubbins Yes. (*To the audience*) I told the council to put a sign up saying "Nudist Colony half a mile ahead". (*She chortles*)

Vendetta Bah. I've more to do with my time than stand here listening to an ugly old woman like you. I'm off to find someone pretty to leer at.

He exits L

Granny Gubbins (*to the audience*) Oooh, I say. What a nasty man. He's exactly the type who'd borrow his best friend's car, then send him an e-mail to tell him his air-bag worked. (*Grimacing*) Mind you— he's right about one thing. I'm not as pretty as I used to be. Once upon a time I had dozens of men at my feet. Nowadays, I've only got the chiropodist. (*Sighing*) And that's the trouble, isn't it girls? Men don't want to know you when you're almost thirty.

Mother Shipton enters R. *She is carrying a rose with a long stalk*

Mother Shipton (*kindly*) Such foolish talk. You'll quickly find
When two hearts meet, then love is blind.
It's always been Dame Nature's plan.
That ev'ry maid should find her man.
Granny Gubbins We can find 'em all right, Missis. It's keeping 'em
that's the problem.
Mother Shipton (*smiling*) Beside the Petrifying Well
Outside the cave wherein I dwell
There grows a bush of flowers sweet
Whose perfume fills the cobbled street.
And all who smell its fragrant scent
Do fall in love and live content.
So take this bloom, (*giving Granny the rose*)
And 'neath the nose
Of he you'd love, just waft this rose.
Then instantly his heart is yours.
You'll be the one that he adores.

Mother Shipton exits R

Granny Gubbins (*startled*) Hang on a minute. What if... Ooooh, she's
gone. (*To the audience*) What a funny old woman. (*Looking at the rose*)
She must have been pulling my leg. How can wafting a flower under
somebody's nose make 'em fall in love?

Jingo enters R. *He does not notice Granny Gubbins*

Jingo (*calling*) Hi ya, kids.

Audience respond

Here. I've got to tell you. I've been looking for somewhere to live
now we're being thrown out of the Hall, and I've found a smashing
place in (*local well-to-do district*). Have you been there? It's ever
so posh, isn't it? And talk about clean. There's no graffiti, the streets
get cleaned every morning, and even the pigeons fly upside down.
(*He laughs and sees Granny*) Oh, hallo, Verruca. What are you doing
here?
Granny Gubbins Well—I've just been wondering if I ought to get
married again.
Jingo (*surprised*) Married?

Granny Gubbins Yes. I don't want to leave it too late, do I? After all—there were twenty-seven candles on my last birthday cake.

Jingo Twenty-seven? There were fifty-six on my slice. (*Falling about laughing*) Leave it out, Granny. Who'd want to marry you?

Granny Gubbins (*indignantly*) Well the Mayor of (*local town*) would, for one. (*Smugly*) Only last week he stopped me in the middle of (*local street*) to show me the lining of his mayoral robes. (*She simpers*)

Jingo (*puzzled*) Mayoral robes? Are you sure?

Granny Gubbins Of course, I'm sure. What else could he have been showing me? He'd nothing else on.

Jingo (*after reacting*) I don't believe a word of it. You're trying to make me jealous, aren't you? (*Firmly*) Well it's not going to work. I'm not a complete idiot, you know. (*He sticks his nose in the air*)

Granny Gubbins Which bits are missing, then? (*She suddenly remembers the rose and wafts it under Jingo's nose*)

Jingo (*reacting instantaneously; dreamily*) Ooh. Ooooh. Oooooooooh. (*Looking at Granny Gubbins*) What a beautiful looking woman. (*He drools at her and paws the ground*)

Granny Gubbins (*delightedly*) Oooh, I say. It worked. He's fallen madly in love with me.

Jingo (*eagerly*) Come here and give me a kiss. (*He puckers his lips at her*)

Granny Gubbins (*protesting*) Just a minute. Just a minute. (*Coyly*) I can't do it here. Not in front of (*charity shop*) and all these people.

Jingo Well if you won't kiss me in front of it, we'll nip round the back and you can kiss me behind.

He hurries her off L and she tosses the rose aside as she gleefully exits

As they vanish from view, Sir Walter enters R

Sir Walter (*to the audience*) I can't believe my eyes, I saw what she did with that rose. It must be a magic one. (*Hurrying over and picking it up*) I wonder if it'll work for anybody? (*Musing*) Just think. If I waved it under Lady Joan's nose, she'd fall in love with me and I could get my hands on every penny of her incredible fortune. (*Thoughtfully*) I'll try it out on the next girl to come along. (*He moves US to the lane cloth and waits*)

A village girl enters L and crosses as though to exit R

Quickly, he jumps forward and wafts the rose under her nose

Girl (*annoyed*) How dare you? Don't you know I'm allergic to pollen? (*She stamps hard on his foot and storms off* R)
Sir Walter (*reeling*) Owwwww. (*Hopping around in anguish*)

Vendetta enters L, *laughing*

Vendetta I saw that. She stamped on your foot, didn't she?
Sir Walter (*scowling*) Yes. But I don't know why. I did exactly what Granny Gubbins did.
Vendetta And what was that?
Sir Walter This. (*Wafting the rose under Vendetta's nose*)
Vendetta (*swooning*) Ooooooh. What a sexy looking man.

Sir Walter looks horrified

Quick. Give me a kiss. (*He puckers up his lips*)

Sir Walter lets out a yell of alarm and rushes off R *chased by an amorous Vendetta*

The Lights fade rapidly

SCENE 3

The Wantley Fayre

Backdrop depicts a huge fairground with ferris wheel, roller coaster, swings, slides and roundabouts, etc. Entrances and exits are concealed by partial views of red and white striped tents or gnarled trees

It is a bright and sunny day, with tray-carrying vendors displaying their various goods as Lady Joan leads the Villagers in singing a lively song

Song 6

At the end of the song, Squire Benjamin enters UR, *and moves quickly down* C *to join Joan*

The Villagers and vendors move U *to listen*

Squire Benjamin (*relieved*) Thank goodness you're all safe. I was scared it may have come this way.

Lady Joan (*puzzled*) What had?
Squire Benjamin The dragon, of course. I went to look at its nesting place, but
   when I got there, it was gone. It must be looking for food.
Villager Two (*horrified*) Oh, no. It might be eating my chickens.

He/She hurries off

Villager Three (*aghast*) Or my sheep.

He/She hurries off

Villager Four Quick, everyone. Back to the village.

*With much commotion the Villagers and vendors exit variously, leaving
Squire Benjamin and Joan alone*

Squire Benjamin (*despondently*) If only I'd got there sooner. I might have been
   able to follow it.
Lady Joan (*kindly*) It's not your fault, Benjamin. You did your best. And
   looking on the bright side, it could have gone for good.
Squire Benjamin (*glumly*) Not according to Mother Shipton. Unless someone
   kills it, it'll be here forever.
Lady Joan (*stoutly*) Then I'll help you look for it. After all, if it's only a baby,
   it can't have gone too far. We'll find it in no time.
Squire Benjamin I hope so. The last thing we need in Wantley is a fully-grown
   dragon. Goodness knows what'd be left by the time it'd done its worst.
   (*Taking her hand*) Come on. We'll start by searching the old farm buildings.

They exit quickly DL

As they do so, Granny Gubbins enters UR *in a dazzling new gown. She moves
down centre, face flushed with excitement*

Granny Gubbins Oh, I say, girls I must tell you. Forget tea and coffee
   in the interval. Get yourselves one of those magic roses. (*Beaming*)
   What a time I had last night with Jingo. (*Peering round cautiously to
   ensure no-one can overhear*) We'd just finished having dinner, when I
   noticed him looking at me again and licking his lips. "Hallo," I
   thought, "He's after another kiss. I'll play hard to get." But the
   next minute, he'd jumped over the table, sent everything crashing to
   the floor, pressed me tightly to his bosom and started making mad
   passionate love to me. (*Simpering*) Ooooh, it was wonderful.
   (*Reflecting*) Mind you—I don't think the manager of (*local*

restaurant)'ll let us in there again. (*Beaming*) Still... Now I'm going to be bridalized, I thought I'd buy a few things for my trousseau. (*Earnestly*) And it's just the place to come, you know. The Annual Goose Fayre. You can buy anything here. (*Confidentially*) There's even a stall where everything on it's been made by prisoners from the local jail. Yes. And talk about quality. I said to the Governor "It's the best stall I've ever seen." "That's because we're very modern, in our jail," he said proudly, "We teach them to make interesting things that people want to buy. Like jewellery, pottery, painting and woodcarving." "And what about hanging baskets?" I said. "Oh, no," he said, "Not any more. These days we let 'em off with a caution."

Jingo enters R, wearily

Jingo (*to the audience*) Hi ya, kids.

Audience respond

Granny Gubbins (*concerned*) What's the matter with you? You look terrible.
Jingo (*mournfully*) I know. I've been awake all night. I think I've got insomnia...
Granny Gubbins Well, that's nothing to look miserable about. I know the perfect cure for insomnia.
Jingo (*hopefully*) Do you?
Granny Gubbins (*firmly*) Yes. You need lots of sleep.
Jingo No, no, Verruca. I've got to see a doctor.
Granny Gubbins Well in that case, you'd better see (*local doctor*) Absolutely marvellous, he is. When my fifth husband was dying of constipation, he couldn't have done more for him.
Jingo (*puzzled*) Constipation? You can't die from constipation.
Granny Gubbins (*firmly*) Well my husband did. But doctor (*repeating the doctor's name*) gave him a prescription for some really, really strong medicine to try and save him.
Jingo (*dolefully*) Yes. But it didn't work, though, did it?
Granny Gubbins (*indignantly*) Of course it worked. (*Proudly*) He went three times before he died. (*Remembering*) And five times after.

Jingo reacts

Anyway, if all you're worried about's not being able to sleep, why don't you do what I do and get a really boring book out of the library? That'll do the trick.

Jingo (*firmly*) No fear. I'm not going in that place again. They're money mad, those librarians.

Granny Gubbins (*puzzled*) Money mad?

Jingo Yes. You know that nice lady who stamps all the books? The one who was expecting a baby?

Granny Gubbins What about her?

Jingo Well she had it last month and it was two weeks overdue. So they fined her sixty p.

Granny Gubbins (*after a reaction*) Well never mind librarians. (*Simpering at him*) Now you're here, we can find out if we're going to be happy together once we're married.

Jingo (*puzzled*) How do we do that?

Granny Gubbins By going to see the fortune-teller in that tent over there (*indicating off*) and asking him to look in his crystal ball. (*Delightedly*) I saw him polishing it this morning. It's this big (*demonstrating*) with holes drilled in the bottom of it. (*She beams happily*)

Jingo (*scornfully*) Holes? Don't be daft, Verruca. They don't have holes in crystal balls.

Granny Gubbins No. Not usually. But if nobody wants their fortunes told, he gives ten-pin bowling lessons, instead.

Jingo (*dismissively*) Well you can get your fortune told, but I'm not wasting my money. If Squire Benjamin can't find a way to kill that dragon, we're going to need every penny we can get.

Granny Gubbins (*remembering*) Oooh, I'd forgotten about that. I wonder how he's doing?

There is a flash

Mauxalinda appears L *in a green follow-spot*

Jingo and Granny react

Mauxalinda (*smirking*) Alas, his hopes are all in vain.
              My precious dragon's flown.
              No more a small and helpless beast,
              He'll very soon be fully grown.
              With gnashing teeth, and sulph'rous breath,
              To all he'll bring despair and death,
              Whilst Wantley village quakes and falls
              'Til nothing's left but old stone walls. (*Laughs nastily*)

Jingo (*to Granny*) Blimey. It's Anne Robinson. (*Or some other caustic tongued personality*)

Mauxalinda (*with menace*) Each morning at some early hour,

> Six pretty maids he shall devour,
> Whilst ev'ry evening, rain or shine,
> On six young men he'll swiftly dine.
> In short... the end is nigh for you.
> (*Sneering*) So now, my friends, a fond adieu.

She gives a mocking bow and exits L, *laughing nastily*

The green follow-spot goes out

Granny Gubbins (*shaken*) Oooh, I say. Did you hear that? What are we going to do?

Mother Shipton enters R

Mother Shipton Fear not. The game is not yet lost.
As she'll discover to her cost.
I bring good news. Your doubts dispel...
(*Beaming*) A way I've found to break her spell.
Granny Gubbins (*relieved*) Thank goodness for that.
Mother Shipton If Squire Ben's heart is fierce and strong.
Right still shall triumph over wrong.
And in the twinkling of an eye,
The dragon will concede or die.
Jingo (*unconvinced*) Yes, but you'll have to find it first. Haven't you heard? It's done a runner.
Mother Shipton No matter. With our help he'll trace
That fearsome monster's hiding place,
And with a few determined blows
Will put an end to all your woes.
Jingo (*worried*) What do you mean? With our help? I haven't got time to go looking for dragons. I've just got myself a new job.
Granny Gubbins (*surprised*) Have you?
Jingo Yes. (*Naming local council*)'s Health and Safety Officer's asked me to do an urgent job for him that'll help stop vandalism.
Granny Gubbins What is it?
Jingo Putting reinforced glass in all the fire alarm boxes.

Granny reacts

Mother Shipton (*sternly*) Unless that dragon's found and slain,
All tasks you do will be in vain.
If Squire Benjamin you claim as friend,
To his search now, you must attend.

Jingo (*reluctantly*) Oh, all right, then. But don't blame me if we can't find it. My sight's gone all funny since I fell off Radish this morning. All I can see is spots before my eyes.
Granny Gubbins Haven't you seen an optician?
Jingo No. Only spots.

Granny pushes him in annoyance

Mother Shipton (*sharply*) Enough. No time for childish play,
                   We really must be on our way.
                   Each passing hour the dragon's strength
                   Grows faster than its scaly length,
                   And lest it very quickly perish,
                   Say "Farewell" to all you cherish.

Mother Shipton exits R

Granny and Jingo hastily follow her

As they do so, Sir Walter enters UL, *followed by Rags and Tatters*

Sir Walter (*fuming*) Bah. I've a good mind to close the fayre down. That knife thrower's the worst act I've seen in my life.
Rags (*scornfully*) Yes. Fifteen knives he threw at that girl and didn't hit her once.
Tatters (*remembering*) My Uncle Fred nearly got a job as a knife-thrower. But somebody beat him to it, so the man who owned the fairground asked if he'd like to be a human cannonball, instead.
Rags And what did he say?
Tatters What do you think? They offered him a thousand pounds a week.
Sir Walter (*startled*) A thousand pounds a week. (*Suddenly very interested*) So your uncle's a very rich man, is he?
Tatters (*grimacing*) Oh, no. No. He was hired and fired on the same night.

Sir Walter glowers and Rags pushes Tatters angrily

Sir Walter (*grimly*) One more joke like that, and you'll be looking for a job yourself. (*Firmly*) Now keep quiet and listen to me.

Rags and Tatters lean in eagerly to listen

    As Mayor of Wantley, I'm the one the villagers should be hailing as a hero. Not that smug-looking, pasty-faced, Squire Benjamin. If he does kill the dragon, it'll be him they'll all be cheering, while I'm left twiddling my thumbs in Humbug Hall.

Rags (*sagely*) You're right there, boss.

Tatters (*agreeing*) They could kick you out and make him mayor.

Sir Walter (*aghast*) Never. (*Craftily*) Because here's what you're going to do. You're going to follow him everywhere he goes, and the minute the dragon's dead, you'll arrest him for cruelty to animals and lock him in old village dungeons.

Rags (*puzzled*) I didn't know we had any old village dungeons.

Tatters (*agreeing*) Me, neither.

Sir Walter (*smirking*) Of course you don't. But we do have them. (*Proudly*) When I built Humbug Hall, many years ago, I built it right on top of them. The only way to reach them is through a secret panel and down a stone staircase. Most of the villagers don't even know they exist, so when he goes missing, they'll never think to look for him there.

Rags But what if he gets away?

Sir Walter (*firmly*) Impossible. I can keep him locked up, forever. Spread the news that he was eaten by the dragon, and tell everyone that I killed it. (*Smirking*) After all—my ancestors were all great hunters. One of them went to Africa to shoot elephants.

Rags (*impressed*) And did he do it?

Sir Walter (*embarrassed*) Unfortunately, no. He gave himself a hernia, carrying the decoys. (*Recovering*) But never mind all that. (*Firmly*) Tonight I shall hold a fancy dress party at Humbug Hall and tell everyone the good news. With the dragon and that interfering Squire Benjamin out of the way, Lady Joan will be only too pleased to accept my proposal of marriage. (*Smirking*) Then every penny of her considerable fortune will go straight into my pockets. (*He chortles*)

Rags (*eagerly*) Does that mean we'll get paid?

Rags and Tatters look at him hopefully

Sir Walter (*sourly*) Do you two think about nothing but money? (*Primly*) It can't buy happiness, you know.

Tatters Who cares? We like money far more than we like happiness.

Song 7

As they sing, Sir Walter sidles away and exits un-noticed

At the end of the song, they realize he is missing and hurry off after him, calling

Lights fade rapidly

SCENE 4

At the edge of the Great Forest

A lane scene. Backdrop of fields and a forest

Madge enters R, *carrying a wicker shopping basket, contents covered by a soft cloth*

Madge (*unhappily*) Oooh, I don't mind being a servant and running errands for Lady Joan, but it's not right Sir Walter sending me out to pick mushrooms for him. Especially with a dragon on the loose. (*Sighing deeply*) Besides—I haven't seen a mushroom all day and it'll be dark, soon. If only I knew where to look. (*Looking off* R, *hopefully*)

Vendetta enters L

Vendetta (*seeing Madge*) Aha. (*To audience*) Now here's a tasty dish for my precious dragon. It's time he got his teeth into something a bit more solid. (*Chuckling nastily*) I'll lure her to his hiding place and serve her up for supper. (*Clearing his throat*) A-hem.

Madge turns to see him

(*Oozing charm*) Greetings, dear lady, (*Bowing deeply*) May I be of assistance? (*Leering at her*)
Madge Only if you know where I can find some big fat mushrooms for Sir Walter's supper. I haven't seen any around here.
Vendetta (*grandly*) Then your search is over. I know the perfect place. Just come along with me and I'll show you. (*Indicating* L)
Madge Oooh. Thank goodness for that. And if you help me fill this basket, I'll give you a great big juicy kiss. (*She flutters her lashes at him*)
Vendetta (*recoiling*) No need for that, Madam. I've never been kissed in my life.
Madge (*surprised*) Haven't you?
Vendetta (*scowling*) No. And no flirtatious female's getting the chance to smear her lipstick on my handsome face.

Madge (*brightly*) Oh, you wouldn't have to worry about that. I'd kiss you without touching you.

Vendetta (*scornfully*) Don't be ridiculous. How could you kiss me without touching me?

Madge Easily. (*Getting out a five pound note*) And I bet you five pounds I can prove it. (*Beaming*)

Vendetta (*interested*) Very well, then. (*He gets a five pound note out*) Here's my five pounds. And the minute you've lost your money, it's straight to the mushroom field.

Madge puts her basket down, grabs Vendetta and kisses him passionately. He vainly tries to break her embrace and struggles wildly. Finally she releases him and he falls to the ground in a heap

Madge (*satisfied*) There. How about that?

Vendetta (*weakly*) But you did touch me. You did. (*Snarling*) And you've lost your five pounds.

Madge (*cheerfully*) I know. (*Grinning*) But boy, was it worth it!

She grabs her basket and exits R happily, tossing the five pound note down as she does so

Vendetta (*furious*) Aaaagh. Come back.

Vendetta scrambles to his feet and chases after Madge and exits R

Squire Benjamin and Lady Joan enter L and move C

Squire Benjamin (*despondently*) It's no use, Joan. We've searched everywhere, but there isn't a trace of the dragon. Where on earth can it be?

Lady Joan (*helpfully*) It could have flown into the forest.

Squire Benjamin (*sighing*) That's true. And if it has, then I'm never going to find it. Those trees go on for miles.

Lady Joan Perhaps Mother Shipton can help. You did say she'd be back if she could find a way to help us.

Squire Benjamin (*brightening*) You're right. If anyone can find where it's hiding, it has to be her. Now why didn't I think of that?

Lady Joan (*smiling*) I'm sure you would have if you hadn't been so worried.

Squire Benjamin (*ruefully*) No. I'd have just gone on searching, and hoping my luck would change. (*Fervently*) Oh, Joan... Thank goodness you're with me. Without you, I'd be nothing but an impoverished Squire with only a suit of clothes to my name. But with you beside me, I'm the luckiest man in the whole wide world.

Song 8

At the end of the song, they move R *to exit*

Now let's find Mother Shipton.

They exit R *and as they do so*

Rags and Tatters furtively enter L

Rags (*looking off* R) There they go. Back toward the village.

Tatters (*relieved*) Thank goodness for that. It'll be dark soon and I don't want to be late getting home.

Rags (*puzzled*) Why not?

Tatters (*embarrassed*) Well — me and the wife used to argue a lot, so we went to one of those marriage guidance places to get some advice on what to do about it.

Rags (*curious*) And what did they tell you?

Tatters They said we were spending too much time in the house together, and what we needed to do was to put our best clothes on, go to a posh restaurant two nights a week and enjoy some candlelight dinners, a bit of soft music and some really smoochy sexy dancing. (*He demonstrates*)

Rags So are you going do it?

Tatters Yes. She's going on Wednesdays and I'm going tonight.

Rags snatches off his cap and beats Tatters around the shoulders with it

(*Trying to protect himself*) Oww. Oww. Owwww.

Rags (*putting his cap back on*) Now shut up and start thinking. What are we going to do about Squire Benjamin? We can't tell Sir Walter he's killed the dragon if he hasn't found it yet.

Tatters (*sighing unhappily*) We'd better keep following him, then. But I hope he hurries up because I've had nothing to eat all day, and I'm absolutely starving.

Rags (*surprised*) What do you mean, starving? What happened to that packet of kipper and garlic sandwiches you brought to work this morning?

Tatters (*grimacing*) I threw 'em away. I can't stand kipper and garlic sandwiches. All those bones in your mouth and the horrible taste. (*Shuddering*) But every day it's the same old thing. Kipper and garlic sandwiches. Kipper and garlic sandwiches. (*Miserably*) I feel sick every time I look at 'em.

Rags (*forcefully*) Well do something about it, then. Tell your missis to make you something else for a change.

Tatters (*puzzled*) But it's nothing to do with her. I make 'em myself.

Rags snatches off his hat and beats Tatters again

(*Cowering*) Oww. Owww. Owwww.

Rags (*disgusted*) Come on. (*He rams his cap back on*) Before we lose sight of him.

Rags exits R, *followed by a reluctant Tatters*

The Lights fade to Black-out

Scene 5

The Ballroom of Humbug hall

When the scene begins, a fancy dress ball is taking place and the Villagers are singing and dancing

Song/Dance 9

At the end of the song, a smirking Sir Walter enters UL, *and moves* C. *He is in his usual robes*

Sir Walter (*grandly*) Welcome, one and all. Welcome to my fabulous stately home. (*Beaming falsely*) Now before you head for the banqueting room for a generous helping of the finest food you've ever tasted, I'd like to say a few words on behalf of my political party.

All react with dismay and exit quickly

(*Scowling*) Pachydermatous peasants. (*To audience*) The only reason I invited them was to make sure the whole village was here when I announce I've killed the dragon. (*He smirks*) They'll be so grateful, they won't say a word when I put their rents up by fifty percent and increase the Council Tax again. (*Glancing around*) But where are those idiots, Rags and Tatters? I can't announce anything till I know my plan's working. (*Glowering*) I'd better go look for them.

He exits DL

Granny enters UR, *in another bizarre gown and hurries down* C

Granny Gubbins (*flustered*) Oh, I say. Sorry I'm late and all that, but I don't know whether I'm coming or going, right now. (*Explaining*) Well — we've been looking for that dragon all afternoon and there hasn't been a sign of it. I'm starting to think it's a frigment of somebody's menageration. (*Reasonably*) Well, you never know, do you? People are always claiming they've seen strange things knocking about. The Loch Ness Monster, UFO's, abominable snowmen, honest politicians. (*Scornfully*) Well I don't believe any of 'em. They need to see a pie-ciatrist. (*Seriously*) No I'm not joking. I was reading one of those posh newspapers this morning— The Daily Sport—and there was a story in it saying they'd just done another survey on mental health and reckoned one person in three was stark staring mad. (*Incredulously*) Have you ever heard anything like it? One person in three. And it's no use thinking "That can't be true". Just look at the people sitting on either side of you. If they both look normal, it's probably you. (*Sighing*) Still—we're going out again tomorrow, so maybe we'll have better luck, then?

Jingo enters UR *in an outsized, ridiculous fancy dress costume*

Jingo (*moving down* C) Hi ya, kids...

Audience respond

Oooh. I'm really looking forward to this party. It's years since I—— (*noticing Granny for the first time and reacting in surprise*) Verruca. What on earth are you wearing?
Granny Gubbins (*pleased*) Do you like it? (*Displaying it*) I got it in (*local dress shop*). It's what they call an "American dress".
Jingo An American dress?
Granny Gubbins Yes. One Yank and it's off. (*She chortles*)
Jingo But this is a fancy dress party.
Granny Gubbins I know. I know. But by the time I got to the shop, they only had one costume left and wanted twenty pounds for it. (*Huffily*) I wasn't paying that.
Jingo What was it?
Granny Gubbins (*frostily*) A sweeping brush handle and a pot of red paint.
Jingo (*puzzled*) Eh?
Granny Gubbins Yes. "What sort of fancy dress costume is that?" I said to the feller behind the counter. "Well," he said, "It'd be perfect for a woman like you. Put the handle in your mouth, pour the paint over your head, and go to the party as a toffee apple." (*Disgustedly*) Cheeky devil. Whoever heard of a toffee apple winning a prize?
Jingo (*kindly*) Never mind, Verruca. I don't think there'll be prizes at this party.

Granny Gubbins (*ruefully*) There always was when the old Squire gave 'em. (*Dreamily*) I won first prize once and got a world cruise on the QE2.

Jingo (*wrinkling his nose*) Ugh. You wouldn't get me on a boat. I hate things that go up and down. I get really seasick.

Granny Gubbins I know. It was just the same with me. But the Chief Steward gave me a little tip. He said there was nothing to worry about because if ever I felt queasy, all I had to do was clutch something as tightly as I could and the feeling would be gone in a flash...

Jingo And did it work?

Granny Gubbins Yes. Ten minutes after we left Southampton, I dashed up onto the bridge and clutched the Captain. (*She chortles*)

Jingo Yes. And I bet he had something to say.

Granny Gubbins Oh, he did. Yes. He said "Here, here." So I said "Where, where?" (*Chortling*) Mind you—I wasn't impressed with his steering. He couldn't follow his compass to save his life.

Jingo What made you think that?

Granny Gubbins Half an hour later, we passed two furniture vans and a number twelve bus.

Squire Benjamin and Lady Joan enter UR

Squire Benjamin (*seeing them*) Granny Gubbins. Jingo.

They hurry down centre to join the others

Where is everyone? There's not a soul in the village. Don't say they were frightened and ran away?

Jingo (*reassuringly*) No, no. There's nothing to worry about, Squire Benjamin. They're all here. At Sir Walter's fancy dress party.

Lady Joan (*amazed*) Fancy dress party? How can he possibly throw a party whilst the village is being menaced by a dragon? Doesn't he realize the danger we're in?

Jingo (*shrugging*) No use asking me. All I know is, everybody's invited and he wants to tell us something important.

Lady Joan (*annoyed*) Well I'd like to know what's more important than saving everyone from being eaten? (*Concerned*) Unless Mother Shipton's found a way to help us, we've no chance at all.

Granny Gubbins (*quickly*) Oh, you don't have to worry about that, love. She told us she knows exactly how to get rid of it, now.

Squire Benjamin (*delighted*) She does? Then that's the best news we've had today. Where is she?

Jingo Waiting for you up at Moore Hall.

Squire Benjamin Then I'd better get there at once. (*To Joan*) Don't worry

Joan. If Mother Shipton really does know how to kill the dragon, I'll be back as soon as I've done it.

He hurries off R

Granny Gubbins (*to Joan*) And you've just got time to get into a really nice fancy dress costume before Sir Walter sees you.
Lady Joan (*looking off L*) Too late. Here he comes now.

Sir Walter enters UL, scowling, followed by Villagers, UL and UR who remain upstage, chatting animatedly but silently

Granny Gubbins, Jingo and Lady Joan edge slightly R

Madge enters down L

Sir Walter (*moving downstage*) Half the evening gone and those idiotic bailiffs still haven't returned. (*Firmly*) Well I'm waiting no longer. I'll make my announcement now—before they all sneak off with their doggy bags and party favours. (*Loudly*) Ladies and gentlemen.

All stop chatting and turn to him

I have very good news for you. (*He smirks*)
Granny Gubbins (*delightedly*) Ooooh, he's leaving the village.

Everyone looks pleased

Sir Walter (*furiously*) No, I am not.

Everyone looks disappointed

(*Heavily*) The reason you're invited here, is to celebrate my victory over that pathetic little dragon who thought it was going to eat us.

Everyone looks surprised

Jingo (*blinking*) Celebrate your victory. What are you talking about? You've never even seen the dragon.
Sir Walter (*offended*) I beg your pardon. (*Grandly*) As Mayor of Wantley, I felt it my civic duty to defend the village against attack, so the moment I heard of our danger, I donned my best armour, took my sharpest sword, and went out into the countryside to meet it face to face. (*He smirks*)

All look unconvinced

Granny Gubbins (*scornfully*) Give over. You're such a coward, you'd never go near a dragon. No wonder somebody wrote a song about you.
Sir Walter (*puzzled*) Song?
Granny Gubbins Yes. Old Man Quiver.

All but Sir Walter are amused

Sir Walter (*annoyed*) How dare you impugn the veracity of my indisputable assertion? The minute my bailiffs arrive, they'll be only too pleased to confirm my indefatigable confrontation with the beast. (*Slyly*) Why—if only I'd arrived there sooner, I might even have saved the life of Squire Benjamin.

Everyone looks surprised

Lady Joan (*puzzled*) Squire Benjamin?
Sir Walter (*with mock regret*) Alas... He found it just before I did, and before he could draw his sword, it shrivelled him to a cinder with its fiery breath, and swallowed the poor boy whole. (*Dabbing at his eyes*)

Villagers look horrified

Lady Joan (*amazed*) That's not true...
Sir Walter (*ignoring her*) I saw it with my own eyes. (*Proudly*) Which is why I drew my own sword, and plunged it deep into the dragon's heart. (*With great emphasis*) A moment later—it was dead at my feet. (*He strikes a heroic pose*)

Rags and Tatters hurry in L

Rags (*gasping*) Boss. Boss.
Sir Walter (*beaming*) Ah, here they are now. (*To them*) Tell them about the dragon. (*He winks heavily at them*)
Tatters (*gasping*) We've seen it. We've seen it. It's bigger than the Town Hall and your wallet put together.
Sir Walter (*to the others*; *smugly*) You see? They've just been to the taxidermists to have it stuffed.
Rags No, we haven't, Sir Walter. It's stuffing itself.
Tatters Sitting outside the kitchen with its neck through the window, spitting flames onto the bread and turning it into to toast.
Rags Then licking up all the marmalade.

Everyone looks horrified

Sir Walter (*aghast*) You mean it's not dead? (*He whimpers with fear and screws up his face tearfully*) I want my mummy. (*He sucks his thumb*)
Granny Gubbins (*scornfully*) What did I tell you? He's yellower than custard.
Madge (*disgustedly*) The big storyteller.

There is a flash and Mauxalinda enters DL *in a green light, followed by Vendetta*

All react and recoil

Mauxalinda (*coldly*) Quite so. Such lies I've seldom heard.
His claims, of course, are quite absurd.
(*Indicating Sir Walter*) This spineless, shaking,
     quaking man
Could never foil my vengeful plan.
But as reward for this deception,
Someone from this great reception
Shall be first, this very night,
To quench the dragon's appetite.

All react in horror

(*To Vendetta*) So quickly, from this crowd displayed,
Select the fairest Wantley maid.
Granny Gubbins (*fiercely*) Lay one finger on me and I'll scream the place down.

Vendetta moves towards her and she hides behind Jingo who panics. Vendetta grabs Lady Joan and all gasp

Lady Joan (*shocked*) Let go of me. (*Struggling*) Let go.

Vendetta flings her over his shoulder and exits L

(*Calling*) Help. Help.
Mauxalinda (*triumphantly*) And now farewell. From this night on,
The dragon dines till all are gone.

She laughs nastily and exits L

The green light goes out

Jingo (*horrified*) What are we going to do? We can't let the dragon eat Lady
   Joan.

Everyone looks concerned

Granny Gubbins (*valiantly*) Don't worry. The minute Squire Benjamin gets
   back, he'll be after her like a shot. (*Proudly*) He's scared of nothing, that
   man. I've even seen him eat sprouts.
Madge (*anxiously*) But where is he?

   Mother Shipton enters DR

Mother Shipton (*firmly*) On his way. So calm your fears.
                               No need for sighs or useless tears.
                               For aided by my magic book,
                               Into the future I did look,
                               And saw at once the only way,
                               The Wantley Dragon, he could slay.
                               In armour — forged from Sheffield steel —
                               He'll make that monster squirm and squeal.
                               For there's no flame can penetrate.
                               Such suits. He'll quickly seal its fate.
Jingo (*anxiously*) But what about Lady Joan? It's going to eat her for
   supper.
Mother Shipton (*smiling*) No, no. Despite the fairy's boast,
                               The piles of marmalade and toast
                               It's eaten from the kitchen store
                               Have filled it up. It can't eat more.
                               In short, until the morn, at least,
                               She has no cause to fear that beast.

All look relieved

                               So raise the roof with shouts and cheers,
                               As Wantley's champion now appears. (*Indicating* UC)

   Squire Benjamin enters UC *dressed entirely in silver (shirt, tunic, tights, shoes,
   cloak gauntlets, etc.) and carrying a sword*

   All but Sir Walter, Rags and Tatters cheer loudly

Squire Benjamin (*moving down* C; *valiantly*) Dearest friends. Though this may seem our darkest hour—as the old saying goes, "It's always darkest before the dawn." And with Mother Shipton to help me, with any luck, Wantley shall see dawn arrive long before we thought it would. So come. Wish me "God speed" as I go to fight the dragon and rescue Lady Joan. For I promise... (*Raising his sword*) Though p'rhaps to realms unknown I'll hie... My aim shall be—to do or die.

All but Sir Walter, Rags and Tatters cheer loudly

Music begins and Squire Benjamin sings

Song 10

As he does so, Sir Walter, Rags and Tatters exit down L *in disgrace*

If required, others can join in the second verse of the song which should end in a tableau as the Lights fade to Black-out

CURTAIN

ACT II

Scene 1

The Village Square

When the scene begins, Villagers are singing and dancing as they decorate their surroundings with flags, balloons and flower garlands, etc.

Song/Dance 11

At the end of the song, Jingo enters UL *and moves down* C

Jingo (*calling*) Hi ya, kids. (*Looking around in astonishment*) Here. What are you doing?

Villager One (*happily*) Decorating the village, of course.

Jingo (*flabbergasted*) I can see that. But why?

Villager Two Well, now we don't have to worry about being eaten by the dragon, we thought we'd have a party to celebrate.

All agree with nods and smiles

Jingo (*concerned*) But it's not dead, yet. We won't know if it is until Squire Benjamin gets back.

Villager Three (*amused*) Of course it's dead. It doesn't stand a chance against Squire Benjamin. If any of us had the slightest doubt, we wouldn't be doing this, would we?

All agree again

Jingo (*doubtfully*) Well I hope you're right. (*Remembering*) But if you are going to have a party, try not to make it a loud one. The couple next door to me had one last night and I couldn't sleep a wink. They were singing and shouting and playing loud music till half past four this morning. Talk about inconsiderate. I went round there this morning and complained to them. "Didn't you hear me banging on the wall last night?" I said. "Oh, I shouldn't worry," the woman said, "We were making plenty of noise ourselves."

Villager One (*kindly*) Never mind, Jingo. As soon as it's dark, all our singing and dancing will be over.

Jingo (*pleased*) Will it?

Villager Two Yes. We'll be watching the firework display and listening to the (*local church*) bell ringers doing their celebration peal.

Jingo reacts

The Villagers laugh and exit variously L *and* R

Jingo (*wearily*) I might have guessed. (*Brightening*) Still if they're having a party, there'll be nobody around to disturb me while I finish inventing my new aftershave lotion. (*Remembering*) Oh, I haven't told you about that, have I? I got the idea last night. (*Confidentially*) I'm going to call it Dragon's Blood — and it'll drive women crazy. I'm making it smell like credit cards. (*Seriously*) Well, you've got to keep up to date, haven't you? I mean— we're all modern, nowadays. You can't live without your laptops, iPods, mobile phones or fax machines, can you? Mind you—some of them are really dangerous. A friend of mine caught his tie in a fax machine last week, and two minutes later he was in Egypt. (*Curiously*) Have you been there? To Egypt?

Audience respond and he shakes his head

I can't understand it. Why do people go to Egypt to look at a dead civilization? They should go to (*local town or district*).

Madge enters UL, *looking upset*

Madge Oh, Jingo. I'm so worried. What am I going to do if Squire Benjamin doesn't save Lady Joan? I'll have to look for another job.

Jingo (*valiantly*) Don't worry, Madge. 'Course he'll save her. One whack with his sword and we'll be laughing. (*Airily*) Mind you if it hadn't been for me, he wouldn't know how to use a sword.

Madge (*surprised*) I didn't know you knew anything about fighting.

Jingo (*proudly*) Oh, yes. I was a soldier in the last war. Fighting for dear life. And look at the country now. The cost of living's never been dearer.

Madge (*swooning*) Ooooh, Jingo. You're such a hero. I've a good mind to give you a great big juicy kiss. (*She puckers her lips at him*)

Jingo (*alarmed*) You'd better not. Verruca might see you and get the wrong idea.

Madge No, she wouldn't. How could she see me if I'm not here?

Jingo (*puzzled*) What do you mean, not here? Of course, you're here.

Madge No, I'm not. And I bet you five pounds I can prove it.

Jingo I bet you can't.

Madge All right then. (*Getting a five pound note out of her cleavage*) Here's my five pound note.

Jingo (*getting a five pound note from his pocket*) And here's mine.

They put their money on the floor downstage, between them

Madge (*beaming*) Now... I'm not in Blackpool, am I?

Jingo (*puzzled*) No.

Madge And I'm not in Brighton?

Jingo Of course not.

Madge Well if I'm not in Blackpool and I'm not in Brighton, I must be somewhere else, mustn't I?

Jingo (*confused*) Well—yes. I suppose you must be.

Madge And if I'm somewhere else, I can't be here, can I? So I win the five pound note.

She picks up the money and exits happily down L

Jingo (*stunned*) Well I'll go to the foot of our stairs. She's diddled me out of a fiver. (*Concerned*) Ooooh. I'll have to get it back or I won't be able to pay my rent. (*Suddenly*) I know... I'll try the same trick on the next one to come along. (*Peering off* R)

Sir Walter enters DL, *scowling. He fails to notice Jingo*

Sir Walter (*furiously*) Bah. Thanks to that incompetent Squire, I'm the laughing stock of the village. And not only that, the town councillors have decided to offer ten thousand pounds to anyone who does kill the dragon. I'm so furious, I've a good mind to go down to the village pond and shout "Orange Sauce" at the ducks. (*Seeing Jingo*) And what's that idiot doing over there? (*He calls*) I say. You there. What do you think you're doing?

Jingo ignores him and Sir Walter scowls again, crosses, and taps him on the shoulder

Jingo (*turning to him in mock surprise*) Oh, hallo, Sir Walter. I didn't know you were here.

Sir Walter (*nastily*) Didn't you hear me calling?

Jingo Well—yes. But I didn't think you were calling me.

Sir Walter (*scowling*) Why not?

Jingo Because I'm not here.

Sir Walter (*sourly*) I know you're not all there. But what are you talking about? Of course you're here. I'm looking right at you.

Jingo Ah—but that's where you're wrong, you see. I'm not here at all. And I can prove it to you.

Sir Walter (*snapping*) Don't be ridiculous.

Jingo All right, then. I bet you five pounds I can prove I'm not here.

Sir Walter Done.

Jingo (*aside*) And you will be. (*Getting his money out*) Here's my five pounds, then. (*He puts it down on the floor*)

Sir Walter (*smirking*) And here's mine. (*He gets his money out and puts it down*)

Jingo Now I'm not in Blackpool, am I?

Sir Walter (*disgustedly*) Of course you're not in Blackpool.

Jingo And I'm not in Brighton?

Sir Walter (*aside*) More's the pity (*To him*) No! You're not in Brighton, either...

Jingo So if I'm not in Blackpool and I'm not in Brighton—I must be somewhere else, mustn't I?

Sir Walter (*impatiently*) Of course you must. Any idiot knows that.

Jingo Exactly. And if I'm somewhere else, I can't be here, can I? So I win the money.

He snatches up the notes and exits R, quickly

Sir Walter (*irate*) Bah. I've been swindled. (*Grimly*) I've just got to get my money back. (*Smirking*) I know... I'll play the same trick on the next one to come along.

Madge enters L

(*Spotting her*) The very person. (*To her*) Margery, my dear how very nice to see you.

Madge (*surprised*) Eh?

Sir Walter I should have seen you before, of course, but the truth of the matter is... I'm not really here. (*He beams at her*)

Madge (*glancing at audience, then smiling at him innocently*) Aren't you?

Sir Walter (*airily*) No. I'm not here at all. And I can prove it.

Madge (*after glancing at the audience again*) You're pulling my leg.

Sir Walter Not at all. (*Aside*) I couldn't even lift it. (*Beaming at her*) And if you'd care to bet me five pounds, I'll prove it to you.

Madge All right, then. (*Getting out a five pound note*) Here's my five pounds.

Sir Walter (*getting his money out*) And here's mine.

They put their money down

Now then... I'm not in Monte Carlo, am I?

Madge Don't you mean Blackpool?

Sir Walter (*snapping*) Don't be ridiculous. Of course, I don't mean Blackpool. Councillors in my position don't go to Blackpool. We go to exotic and exclusive places abroad and put it down as expenses. Now stop interrupting and answer my question. I'm not in Monte Carlo, am I?

Madge (*meekly*) No.

Sir Walter And I'm not in Jamaica.

Madge You're not. You're right.

Sir Walter (*smirking*) So if I'm not in Monte Carlo and I'm not in Jamaica, then I must be somewhere else, mustn't I?

Madge (*nodding*) You must, Sir Walter. You must.

Sir Walter (*triumphantly*) And if I'm somewhere else, I can't possibly be here. So I win the money. (*Falling about laughing*)

Madge picks up the notes

(*Surprised*) Here... What are you doing? That money's mine.

Madge But it can't be yours, Sir Walter. You've just told me. You're not here.

She exits R quickly

Sir Walter shrieks with rage, chases after her and exits

Granny enters UR in another extravagant costume and moves down centre

Granny Gubbins (*beaming*) Oh, I say—you'll never guess what, boys and girls. (*Chortling*) I've just been having my picture painted. (*Proudly*) By Mr Picasso. Yes. The famous Pablo Picasso. It's the first painting he's done since somebody mugged him in (*local street*). The police asked him to do a sketch of the feller who hit him and the next day they arrested three suspects: a fried egg, the London Eye and a packet of Dolly Mixtures. But you've got to speak as you find, haven't you? And he's ever so nice. He said he'd paint me anyway I liked. Well... I thought about it for a minute, then I asked him if he'd mind painting me in the nude. (*Simpering coyly*) "Of course, I will," he said, "But I'll have to leave my socks on or I'll have nowhere to keep the brushes." Mind you—it looked a bit funny when he'd finished it. I said "I'm not sure it really does me justice." Well, he looked me up and down for a second or two then said " I should forget justice, love. You're more in need of mercy." (*Beaming*) Still—it'll look lovely on the living room wall when me and Jingo get married. (*Remembering*) And that reminds me. I've not seen him since last night. I hope he's not gone fighting that dragon with Squire Benjamin.

Rags and Tatters enter UL, *looking unhappy*

(*Spotting them*) Oooh, I wonder if they've seen him? (*Brightly*) Hallo,
boys.

Rags (*mournfully*) Hallo, Granny.

Granny Gubbins (*concerned*) What's the matter? Don't say there's been
bad news?

Tatters (*grimacing*) There has for us. Thanks to that boss of yours not killing
the dragon, Sir Walter's given us the sack.

Rags Yes. So now we've no jobs and we're flat broke.

Granny Gubbins Well it serves you right for working for him. (*Primly*) You
wouldn't catch me doing it. (*Smugly*) I've just been offered a job at the (*local*)
bowling alley.

Tatters Tenpin?

Granny Gubbins No. Full time. But once the dragon's dead and Squire
Benjamin collects the reward, he can pay the council tax he owes and I'll get
my old job back at Moore Hall.

Rags (*dully*) Oh, no you won't. Not while Sir Walter's got the title deeds.

Granny Gubbins (*surprised*) Eh?

Tatters (*scowling*) He found 'em in a chest of drawers he bought from Squire
Benjamin, so everything's his now.

Granny Gubbins (*indignantly*) Over my red body. He's not getting his measly
mucky maulers on Squire Benjamin's stately home. (*Grimly*) If he puts a toe
of his size fifteens inside it, I'll chop his head off and throw it in his face.

Rags Fat chance of that. Unless he gives 'em back, it doesn't matter how
many dragons Squire Benjamin kills. Moore Hall's gone for good.

Granny Gubbins (*thoughtfully*) Then we've got to find a way to get our hands
on 'em. (*Frustrated*) Ooooh. If only we knew a burglar.

Tatters (*remembering*) I don't know about a burglar, but my Uncle Alfie used to
be a pickpocket. (*Proudly*) He was known as the One Fingered Wonder.

Rags One Fingered Wonder? Don't be so stupid. What could a pickpocket
steal if he only had one finger?

Tatters (*defensively*) Polo mints.

Rags snatches off his cap and beats Tatters, angrily

Owww, Owww. Owwww. (*Trying to cover himself*)

Granny Gubbins (*annoyed*) Oh, stop it, you two. We need to consecrate.

Rags replaces his cap sulkily

(*Firmly*) Now here's what we have to do. (*Glancing round to see no-one else
is listening*) We sneak into Humbug Hall, get Madge to find those title deeds

and snaffle 'em before he even knows they're gone.

Rags (*worried*) But what if we get caught? We could be thrown in jail for being crooks.

Tatters (*dismissively*) No, we couldn't. They don't know what to do with crooks, these days. All the jails are full.

Granny Gubbins Yes. And so are the Houses of Parliament. Now stop making excuses and let's get on with it. (*Firmly*) From now on we're working together.

Song 12

At the end of the song they all exit DL

The Lights fade rapidly

Scene 2

A path through the woods, a lane scene

Vendetta enters R, *pulling Lady Joan behind him*

They move C

Lady Joan (*struggling*) Let go of me. Let go.

Vendetta (*sniggering*) Oh, no, my pretty one. We can't take the risk of you escaping. Think how disappointed the Dragon would be. He's eaten nothing but toast and marmalade since hatching, so the sight of you will soon have him licking his lips. (*He laughs nastily*)

Lady Joan (*defiantly*) As if I cared about your stupid dragon. I'd sooner face him than spend another minute in your company.

Vendetta (*balefully*) Yes. You say that now, but wait till you hear his mighty roars. Wait till you see his yellow eyes and razor-sharp teeth. Wait till you see his scaly skin and feel his fiery breath scorching you. (*Chuckling*) Then you'll be trembling with fear.

Lady Joan (*icily*) That's what you think. The minute Squire Benjamin arrives, it'll wish it had never been born. And so will you.

Vendetta (*scornfully*) Squire Benjamin. (*Laughing*) Just let him set foot near the dragon's cave and it's the last thing he will do. With the magic of Mauxalinda to protect us, nothing can save Wantley from ruin. Especially a penniless Squire with a puny sword. Now come—the dragon awaits.

He drags the struggling Joan off L

Mother Shipton appears R *and watches them go*

Mother Shipton You count your chicks before they're hatched.
Against my second sight you're matched
And though, for now, perhaps it seems
No chance we have 'gainst fairy schemes,
With luck, you'll find to your dismay
A different ending to this day.

She exits R

Radish pokes his head round the proscenium arch, L. *Seeing no-one is there, he enters and moves jauntily* R *as though to exit*

Squire Benjamin (*off* R) Radish? Radish?

Radish stops, turns, and begins to tiptoe quickly towards the exit L

Squire Benjamin enters R, *sword in his belt, and sees him with relief*

Oh, there you are.

Radish slumps, then turns to him

(*Crossly*) Why did you run away like that? (*Moving to him*) How can I fight the dragon and rescue Joan if I don't have you to ride on?

Radish whispers to him

(*Frowning*) You don't believe in fighting?

Radish shakes his head then whispers to him again

(*Puzzled*) It's against your religion?

Radish nods

And what religion's that?

Radish whispers to him

You're a devout coward?

Radish nods

(*Amused*) No, you're not, Radish. You may be old, but you're the bravest horse I know.

Radish shakes his head

(*Insisting*) Yes, you are. You're the bravest horse in the world and I couldn't possibly face the dragon without you to help me.

Radish looks embarrassed at the praise

Now stand still and let me get up on your back.

Radish immediately closes up

(*Surprised*) What's the matter?

Radish whispers to him

You don't want me to fall off, because I might break a leg?

Radish nods

(*Amused*) But of course I won't fall off. And why should it worry you?

Radish whispers

Because you saw a terrible accident at the races last week?

Radish nods

(*Concerned*) What happened?

Radish whispers

A jockey fell and broke his leg—and the vet had to shoot him. (*Laughing*) Oh, Radish. I don't believe a word of it.

Radish assumes his normal position

(*Sternly*) Now let's get on with finding the dragon's lair. It'll be morning soon and we've got to get there before he starts feeling hungry and eats Joan. (*Sighing*) If only I felt more confident of killing it. It's all very well wearing a suit of armour and carrying a sword, but if everything we've been told about the dragon's true, it's not going to be easy.

Radish whispers to him

You're feeling a bit nervous?

Radish nods and his knees begin to knock

(*Nodding*) And so am I. But when I was small, dear old Granny Gubbins told me just what to do at moments like this. Would you like to hear it?

Radish nods hastily

Then you shall.

Song 13

At the end of the song, they exit jauntily L

The Lights fade rapidly

SCENE 3

Mayor's Parlour

Maids and footmen are cleaning the room. In the background, some are folding sheets, some are sweeping the floor and others are polishing the silverware. In the foreground, others are dancing to a lively tune whilst holding feather dusters

Dance 14

At the end of the routine, they all exit cheerily

Sir Walter enters R *back, and moves down* C

Sir Walter (*sourly*) Bah. Look at the mess that nauseating rabble left last night. Not a clean corner in the room. I'll have to have it decorated. Now who can I get to do the job?

Madge enters L, *backwards, on tiptoe. She is peering off as though looking for someone, and clutches a white scroll tied with pink ribbon*

(*To audience*) The very person. And as I'm already paying her wages, I'll get everything done for nothing. (*Smirking*) Good morning, Miss Margery.

Madge (*startled*) Oh. (*She turns to him and hides the scroll behind her*) Sir Walter. I thought you were out.

Sir Walter (*remembering and scowling*) Yes. I was. I've just been to (*local travel agents*) to book my next holiday. But I won't be going there again.

Madge (*puzzled*) Why not? They're ever so nice in there.

Sir Walter (*firmly*) Rubbish. I told them I wanted an exclusive hotel in Switzerland, but refused to pay the inflated price they were asking "Not a penny more than twenty pounds," I told them, "And you may as well remember I'm looking for total peace and complete relaxation."

Madge And what did they offer you?

Sir Walter (*scowling*) A jar of Horlicks and a sleeping tablet. (*Brightening*) But enough of this idiopathy. I've a special little job for you. (*Beaming at her*)

Madge (*surprised*) Me?

Sir Walter (*airily*) As my dear ward, Lady Joan, may soon be rescued and return to Humbug Hall—I feel we ought to brighten things up to welcome her. So I'm putting you in charge of organising things (*scowling*)—and expect to see it done by the time I've finished watching (*popular children's television show*).

He exits DL

Madge looks aghast

Jingo enters UR. *He is wearing a garish but quick washable outfit, which should be similar to his usual style of costume*

Jingo (*calling*) Hi ya, kids.

Audience respond

Ooooh, I don't know what's going on, but I got a text message from Verucca saying I had to meet her here — in Sir Walter's Parlour. (*Puzzled*) You've not seen her, have you?

Audience respond

Madge (*worried*) Ooooh, Jingo. (*Hurrying down to him*) What am I going to do?

Jingo (*seeing her*) What's wrong?

Madge Granny Gubbins asked me to find the title deeds belonging to Squire Benjamin. (*Showing the scroll*) But she's not arrived to collect them yet, and Sir Walter's back already. He wants me to decorate this place.

Jingo (*cockily*) Don't worry, Madge. You go find Verucca, and I'll do the decorating. I used to do all the painting and decorating for (*local area*)'s new council houses. Right till the day of the accident.

Madge (*frowning*) What accident?

Jingo The builders took the scaffolding down before I'd time to paper the walls.

Granny Gubbins enters UR *in a new horrendous gown*

Granny Gubbins (*gasping*) Oooooh. Sorry I'm late. But I've just seen a terrible crash.

Madge and Jingo look horrified

This car came racing up (*local street*) at ninety miles an hour, swerved to avoid a dog and went straight through the butcher's window. There was blood and bones everywhere. The wreck was on fire. The driver was unconscious and couldn't get out. Oooooh, it was terrible. And I was the only one who saw it happen. (*Proudly*) Thank goodness I used to be a nurse and had medical training. Everything came back in a flash and I knew exactly what to do.

Jingo What was it?

Granny Gubbins (*with satisfaction*) I sat on the pavement and put my head between my knees to stop myself from fainting. (*She nods firmly for emphasis*)

Madge (*worried*) Well never mind that. Here's the title deeds you wanted. (*Giving her the scroll*) Now you'd better get back to Moore Hall before Sir Walter finds out they're missing.

Granny Gubbins You're right. (*To Jingo*) Come on, trouble. We've got to get these to Squire Benjamin as quick as we can.

Jingo (*protesting*) But I can't, Verucca. I've promised to decorate Sir Walter's parlour so Madge won't get into trouble. Why don't you take her with you?

Granny Gubbins (*unhappily*) Oh, all right but I'll send Rags and Tatters in to help you. The quicker it's done, the better. Like the old proverb says "Many cooks can lead a horse to water, but you can't turn a rolling stone".

Granny and Madge exit R

Jingo (*to the audience with a sigh of relief*) Thank goodness they've gone, kids. (*Glancing round nervously*) I told a little fib there. I've never papered a room in my life. Especially one as big as this. I don't know where to start.

Rags and Tatters enter UR

They are carrying a long, solid table that has a large book on top of it, plus several rolls of wallpaper (one in pre-cut lengths), and a large sheet or two to protect the floor. They deposit the table mid-stage c

Rags (*breezily*) Here we are. Rags and Tatters.
Tatters Decorator's assistants *extraordinaire*.

They both bow

Jingo (*disgustedly*) Fat lot of use, you two are going to be. I bet you've never papered a room, either.
Rags No, but we know a man who has. (*Picking up the book*) The man who wrote this book. (*Showing it*)
Jingo (*taking it*) Oh, smashing. I'll just have a quick read and we can start at once.
Tatters And we'll get all the other stuff.

Rags and Tatters exit R

Jingo moves DS

Jingo (*to audience; excitedly*) Oh, it's a great book, this is. (*Reading aloud*) "How to do whitewash jobs and cover things up" by the Prime Minister's personal adviser. Ooooh I can't wait to get started.

Rags and Tatters enter R, *carrying two plastic buckets each. Two contain "paste", one contains "red emulsion paint" and the other is filled with confetti sized scraps of mixed coloured paper and tin-foil, or polystyrene beads. All three "paste" buckets contain paste-brushes*

Rags Back again. (*Moving* L)
Tatters With the paint, hot water, and plenty of wallpaper paste.

They deposit their buckets downstage but in front of the table

Jingo Right. (*Looking inside the book*) Now according to this, the first thing we do is put sheets down to protect the floor.
Rags (*confirming*) Sheets down to protect the floor.
Tatters (*echoing*) Sheets down to protect the floor.

They take the sheets from the table and quickly lay them out in front of it

Jingo (*still reading*) Then we roll out the wallpaper.

Rags (*moving behind the table* L) Roll out the wallpaper.
Tatters (*moving behind the table* R) Roll out the wallpaper.

Rags unrolls a length of paper, holding the roll with one hand, and pulling with the other

Rags (*calling*) Wallpaper unrolled.
Tatters (*echoing*) Wallpaper unrolled.
Jingo (*confirming*) Wallpaper unrolled. (*Looking at the book again*) Now put some paste on it.
Tatters (*to Rags*) Now put some paste on it.
Rags Now put some paste on it. (*Looking round*) Where's the paste?
Jingo Over here. (*He points to it*)
Tatters (*echoing*) Over there. (*He points*)
Rags Right. (*He lets go of the paper and moves* L *round the table to get the paste*)

The paper rolls up again, without anyone noticing. Rags returns behind the table and sees what has happened. Putting the bucket down, he unrolls the paper once again, releases it to pick up the paste brush, and as he does so, the paper rolls up. He stands, sees it and reacts

   I think I need a bit of help.
Tatters (*quickly*) I'll do it. I'll do it.

He moves behind the table and unrolls the paper, holding the right end of it as Rags holds the left end. Once the paper is flat, Rags releases his end to pick up the pastebrush. The paper at once rolls up to meet Tatters' end. Rags stands up again and reacts

Rags (*puzzled*) You must be holding the wrong end. (*Putting the brush back in the bucket*) Try this one.

They change sides and unroll the paper again. Rags lets go to pick up the brush and the paper rolls up towards Tatters. Rags stands up and reacts

Jingo (*disgustedly*) Ooooh, I knew you two were useless. Let me show you how it's done. (*He tosses the book offstage, goes behind the table and positions himself* C) Now then. I'll flatten the paper out, and when I nod my head, put plenty of paste on it.
Rags (*blankly*) Eh?
Tatters (*to him*) When he nods his head, put plenty of paste on it.
Rags (*to Jingo*) Are you sure?

Jingo Of course, I am. (*Spreading out the paper until its flat*) Right. Now quick. Quick. (*Nodding his head rapidly*)

Rags picks up the bucket of "paste" and tips it over Jingo's head

(*Howling*) Aghhhh. Ooooooh. Quick. Give me a cloth.

Jingo blindly grabs at Tatters' shirt and pulls it towards his face. The shirt front rips off exposing Tatters' chest

Tatters Ahhhhhh.

Jingo mops at his face with the shirt front then looks at Tatters' chest

Jingo   Blimey. That's a nasty looking wart you've got on your chest. (*Peering closer*) Ooooh, and there's one on the other side, as well. (*He drops the shirt-front behind the table and turns to Rags in annoyance*) What did you do that for?

Rags (*taken aback*) That's what you told me to do. When you nodded your head, I'd to put plenty of paste on it.

Jingo Not my head, you plonker. I meant the wallpaper. (*Looking at it*) Oh, look at it. It's absolutely ruined now. We'll have to use another piece. (*He screws the paper up, drops it behind the table and picks up a complete roll*) You get hold of this end (*giving the loose end to Rags*) and you get hold of this. (*Giving the roll to Tatters*) Now stretch it out while I get some more paste.

Jingo comes from behind the table to get the second "paste" bucket. As he does so, Rags and Tatters unroll the paper, facing each other, and retreating as they also move downstage. Jingo picks up the bucket and hurries back, not noticing the paper which by now is the width of the stage and taut. He walks straight through it

Rags and Tatters stagger backwards and off, taking their respective pieces of wallpaper with them

Now where've they gone?

They both enter on hands and knees, crawling to C

(*Annoyed*) I wish you'd stop playing about. We'll never get finished at this rate.

All move to behind the table. Jingo C, *once more. He puts the bucket on the floor*

Now let's have another piece of paper.

Rags selects another pre-cut length

Right. (*He flattens it out and turns to Tatters*) Now you hold that end down, (*To Rags*) And you hold the other.

They do so. Both stand at the ends of the table

And we'll put the first piece in the corner over there. (*Stooping to pick up the paste brush*)
Tatters I'll get some steps.

He dashes off R to get them

The paper starts to roll toward Rags, who throws himself full length onto the table, on top of the paper, to push it back. Jingo stands up and without noticing, begins pasting him head to foot with broad strokes

Tatters enters with a tall step-ladder which he places R against a solid wing-flat

As Jingo replaces the brush in the paste, Rags pushes himself off the table to stand again. Jingo picks up an end of the paper, holding it aloft in both hands, and with it held in front of his face, crosses to the ladder. As the front of the paper comes to rest against the Steps, he begins to climb, tearing the paper into shreds with his feet. By the time he gets to the top, all that he carries is a scrap the size of a postcard. He presses it to the solid wing-flat and pats it into place

(*Satisfied*) There. (*Peering at it*) Funny. It seems to have shrunk. (*Disgustedly*) That's the last time I use cheap wall-paper. (*Looking at it again*) Oooh, it's peeling off already. Quick. Quick. Bring me some paste.

Tatters grabs the paste bucket and hurries to the ladder. Holding it firmly in one arm, the lip of the bucket on his right shoulder, he begins to climb. Rags stands at the bottom of the step-ladder to steady it. As Tatters climbs, the bucket tips and the paste covers Rags from head to foot

Tatters (*reaching the top*) Here we are. (*Looking into the bucket*) Oh, it's empty.
Jingo Never mind. I think I've put it upside down, anyway. Let's do another piece.

They descend the ladder then see Rags and react. Gingerly Tatters reaches out and lifts a dab of "paste" from Rags' face with a finger, and tastes it

Tatters (*pulling a face*) Ugh. Vanilla and cauliflower...

Rags (*clearing his face; grimly*) I'll get some more paste.

He moves down to collect the bucket of red liquid as a giggling Jingo and Tatters move behind the table. Rags joins them and puts the bucket down

Jingo Another piece of paper.

Tatters Another piece of paper.

Rags (*getting a pre-cut length*) Another piece of paper.

This is rolled out flat, Rags and Tatters each holding an end whilst Jingo smoothes it from the centre, outwards

Jingo And we'll paste this bit properly. Now watch carefully.

Rags and Tatters lean in to watch as Jingo stoops and straightens holding the paste brush which is loaded with the red liquid. Looking at Rags, he liberally slops the paper with very broad strokes, coating Tatters' face and chest at the same time without realizing it. Jingo suddenly notices the colour and reacts in horror

This isn't paste. It's paint. (*He turns to Tatters and lets out a startled yelp*) Ahhhhh. He's overcome with emulsion.

Rags laughs

Tatters (*annoyed*) Oh. So you think it's funny, do you? Well laugh this off, then.

He crosses behind Jingo and snatches off Rags' hat

(*Turning to Jingo*) Hold that.

Puzzled, Jingo holds the hat, brim uppermost, whist Rags looks on warily. Tatters picks up the bucket, fills the hat with red "paint", then quickly puts the bucket down and takes the hat from Jingo. With a smile of triumph, he rams the hat onto Rags' head and pulls it firmly down. A jet of red liquid shoots into the air through a small hole in the top of the hat, and the rest streams down from beneath it. Jingo and Tatters laugh. Furiously, Rags picks up the bucket and prepares to hurl the contents at Tatters

Jingo (*horrified*) No! No! Stop.

Jingo dashes round Tatters to get between them. Rags hurls the liquid at him by mistake. As all react, they notice the audience laughing

(*Grimly*) Oh. So you think it's funny as well, do you? (*He hurries* DS *grabs the last bucket and heads for the edge of the stage*)

Rags and Tatters watch him in dismay

Well laugh this off.

He hurls the contents into the audience and there is an instant Black-out

SCENE 4

A Rocky Gorge

There is a very loud roar from the dragon in the darkness. As the Lights slowly come up to semi-darkness, it reveals a bleak-looking and sinister gorge. There is another great roar

Mauxalinda enters L

Vendetta enters R, *pulling Joan along by the arm*

On seeing Mauxalinda, he stops and Joan recoils

Mauxalinda (*gloating*) With cold and ever-watchful eye,
I wait, as darkness fills the sky,
And look towards the moment when,
My precious dragon feeds again.

Joan tries to break free but fails

(*Gleefully*) Already he's consumed ten cows,
Four horses, (and the farmer's ploughs),
A flock of sheep, five pigs, a goose,
Two dozen rabbits running loose,
A dog, six cats, a Sunday roast
And stacks of marmalade and toast.
But now it's time, as you'll agree,
To seek the justice due to me.

There is another roar from the dragon and Joan cowers

> (*Soothingly*) Hush, hush, my pet. For very soon
> There'll come the rising of the moon,
> And on the very stroke of nine,
> On humans, at long last, you'll dine.

She laughs in triumph and exits

Vendetta follows her, dragging Joan behind him

Lady Joan (*calling*) Help. Help.

As they exit, Squire Benjamin and Radish enter R

Squire Benjamin (*concerned*) That was Joan's voice. I'd recognize it anywhere. She must be somewhere near. (*He glances round hopefully*)

Mother Shipton enters R

Mother Shipton Just half a league to go, young Squire,
> And there you'll find your heart's desire.
> But don't forget. Some time tonight
> You'll also have to stand and fight.
> So smear your sword, if safe you'd be.
> With juice from yonder berry tree. (*Indicating off* L)
> For not e'en fairy magic can
> Withstand the power of old Rowan.

Squire Benjamin (*gamely*) I'll certainly take your advice... But couldn't you look into the future and see if I do kill the dragon?

Mother Shipton (*sighing*) Alas, my visions come and go.
> Some things, I fear, I'll never know.
> But don't forget, the foe you face
> Could soon eat all the human race.
> So fight with all your might and main
> If homeward you'd return again.

She exits

Squire Benjamin (*heavily*) Well... This looks like it, Radish. In a few more minutes, we'll be meeting the dragon face to face.

Radish trembles as Squire Benjamin turns to the audience

Wish me luck, everybody.

He exits L

Radish looks at the audience, then turns and begins to tiptoe R. *Almost at the exit, he halts, pulls himself together, turns and hurries off after Squire Benjamin*

Madge and Granny Gubbins enter R, *cautiously. Granny Gubbins is wearing another "creation"*

Granny Gubbins (*glancing around*) Oooh, I say... I don't like the look of this place. It reminds me of (*local area*).
Madge It doesn't bother me. I've been here before.
Granny Gubbins (*surprised*) Have you?
Madge Oh, yes. I was walking down this path last week when a strange man came towards me carrying a breeze block, two chickens, a goose and a tin bucket. "Oooh," I said to him, "For one minute, I thought you were going to kiss me before I could run away."
Granny Gubbins (*baffled*) Kiss you? How could he kiss you carrying all those things?
Madge That's what he said. So I told him. Put the goose under the bucket, the breeze block on top to stop it escaping and I'll hold the chickens.
Granny Gubbins Oooh, you're man mad, you are. When I was your age, the only man who'd ever kissed me was my fiasco.
Madge You mean fiancé.
Granny Gubbins I know what I mean. (*Proudly*) He was a musician in the Royal Philharmonic Orchestra.
Madge And did you marry him?
Granny Gubbins (*grimacing*) No. He fell over a drum kit one night, hit his head on a cymbal, banged his nose on a triangle, flattened a tambourine and got rushed into hospital.
Madge Was he badly hurt?
Granny Gubbins No. But he had a severe case of percussion.

Sir Walter enters L

Sir Walter (*spotting them*) Aha. (*Advancing on them*) The very people. Where are those title deeds you stole from Humbug Hall?
Granny Gubbins (*fiercely*) Nowhere you'll ever find them. (*Proudly*) I've got 'em hidden where the hand of man has never set foot and they're going straight back to the feller they belong to. Squire Benjamin. (*Scowling*) And anyway how did you get here?

Sir Walter (*sneering*) I've been following your trail for hours. And if you don't hand over those deeds, I've got no other option but to sue you for every penny you have.

Granny Gubbins (*unfazed*) I haven't got anything. I spent all my money on a new business. I've bought a flock of sheep that've just been crossed with the world's biggest porcupine. (*Thinking*) I don't know what they're going to taste like, but in the meantime, they're knitting their own sweaters.

Sir Walter (*glowering*) Bah. Then as you won't hand them over, I'll return to Wantley at once and arrange to have you banished. (*Awkwardly*) You— er—couldn't lend me the bus fare, could you? I seem to be financially embarrassed at the moment...

Granny Gubbins (*scornfully*) You must be joking. You can walk back.

Sir Walter (*protesting nervously*) But it's getting rather dark. What if I bump into the dragon? Or even worse meet up with a ghost?

Madge (*smugly*) Don't be silly, Sir Walter. There's no such thing as ghosts. Are there, Granny?

Granny Gubbins (*firmly*) Oh, yes there are. I stayed at (*local inn or hotel*) once, and they had ghosts for customers.

Sir Walter What? Who told you that?

Granny Gubbins It was written over the door. (*With drama*) Licenced to serve spirits. And I'll tell you this much for nothing. They could go though any door in there, those spirits. No matter how tightly it was locked.

Madge (*amazed*) How did they do that?

Granny Gubbins They used skeleton keys.

She chortles, and pushes playfully Sir Walter, who is sent staggering R

(*Seriously*) But no. Of course, there're ghosts. Great, horrible, creepy things that'll frighten the life out of you the minute you see them.

Madge You mean like Trinny and Susannah? (*Or another pair of television "personalities"*)

Granny Gubbins (*hastily*) No, no. I wouldn't say ghosts were that bad.

Sir Walter (*anxiously*) But there aren't any ghosts round here, are there?

Granny Gubbins (*shrugging*) I wouldn't be surprised. It's ever so quiet, isn't it? And ghosts like quiet that's why they don't like singing.

Madge (*surprised*) Singing?

Granny Gubbins Didn't you know? (*Airily*) Oh, yes. If ever you want to get rid of a ghost, all you have to do is sing and they'll be off like a rocket.

Sir Walter (*doubtfully*) So if I sing on my way back to Wantley, I've nothing to worry about?

Granny Gubbins Not a thing.

Sir Walter (*almost pleading*) Well, in that case... I wonder if you'd stay here
for a while and listen while I practise. Then if anything horrible does appear,
you'll be able to warn me.

Granny Gubbins Well... I don't know why we should, but go on then. Get your
tonsils in gear— and if we do see anything, we'll tell you.

*Sir Walter clears his throat nervously, and Granny and Madge exchange
sniggers behind his back. He begins to sing in an out of tune manner*

Song 15

A ghost appears L, *and drifts behind all three of them without them noticing*

The ghost exits R

Sir Walter (*finishing*) Was that all right? You didn't see anything, did
you?

Madge (*attempting to keep a straight face*) Not a thing.

Granny Gubbins (*innocently*) Not even a teeny weeny ghost. (*To audience*)
Did we kids?

Audience respond

(*Surprised*) Eh? You did see something? Well what was it?

Audience respond

A ghost? (*She reacts*)

Madge (*alarmed*) Ooo-er. I don't like the sound of that, Granny.

Sir Walter (*trembling*) Neither do I. (*Plaintively*) I want my Mummy. (*Sticking
his thumb in his mouth*)

Granny Gubbins (*bravely*) Well... I think it's gone now, so there's nothing to
worry about.

Madge But what if it comes back and grabs us all?

Granny Gubbins Well I'll tell you what we'll do. We'll all sing Sir Walter's
song and if the ghost does come back, all the boys and girls in the audience can
shout and warn us. (*To the audience*) Will you do that for us?

Audience respond

Madge (*relieved*) Ooooh, I feel a lot safer now. But we'd better start singing
before it's too late.

With a great show of nerves, the trio begin singing

As they sing the ghost re-appears R *and moves behind them to exit* L

As the audience shout, the trio stop singing

Granny Gubbins (*to audience*) What are you shouting for? Did it come back?

Audience respond

Ooooer. Well where is it now?

Audience respond

Madge (*worried*) I think we should take a look.
Granny Gubbins All right, then. We'll go this way.

To the accompaniment of creepy music, with exaggerated caution, they move L *in file and follow round in a circle*

The ghost enters L *and follows Sir Walter until the trio end up where they began. Ghost exits* R

Madge (*disgustedly*) Well I didn't see anything.
Sir Walter Neither did I.
Granny Gubbins Perhaps we should have gone the other way.
Sir Walter Good idea. Follow me.

They repeat the movement, circling to the R

The ghost reappears

The ghost follows Granny, but remains CB *as the others continue to their original positions*

Granny Gubbins Well there was nothing that way either.

Audience continue to shout

Well if we've looked over there (*indicating* L) and seen nothing, and we've looked over there (*indicating* R) and seen nothing... Where do we look next?

Audience respond

Behind us? (*To others*) They say we've got to look behind us.

Madge We'd better do it then. Let's count up to three, then all turn at once, and we'll see if there's anything there.

Together One-two...

The ghost bobs down

Three.

They all turn, look over the ghost, then turn back in disgust

The ghost rises again

Sir Walter (*scowling*) There's nothing there at all. Those idiots in the audience are trying to make fools of us. I'll have them banished from the theatre. Let's start singing again.

They begin singing again. The ghost taps Granny Gubbins on the shoulder

She turns, sees it, screams and hurries off L, *chased by the ghost*

After a moment the others stop singing

Madge (*puzzled*) Granny? (*Looking round*) Granny? (*To audience*) Where's she gone?

Audience respond

The Ghost chased her? Ooo-er.

Sir Walter (*nervously*) We couldn't have been singing loud enough. Let's try again.

They start singing

The ghost enters, moves behind them and taps Sir Walter

Sir Walter turns, sees it, yells and hurries off R, *chased by the ghost*

Madge stops singing and looks round

Madge (*worried*) Sir Walter? Sir Walter? (*To audience*) Don't say the ghost chased him as well?

Audience respond

Oh, no. Now I'll have to sing on my own. (*She nervously begins to sing*)

The ghost enters and taps her on the shoulder

She turns, sees it, then grabs it and gives it a passionate kiss

The ghost breaks free with a scream of fear and races off L

(*To audience*) That'll teach him a lesson.

With a satisfied smirk she exits

The Lights fade

SCENE 5

Outside the dragon's lair

A full set. The backdrop is of gnarled and ancient trees and DL *is the entrance to the dragon's cave, set at the foot of a great cliff. Rocks and trees mask other entrances* L *and* R. *Lighting is gloomy, but a red glow issues from the cave*

Weird creatures are performing a dance outside the cave

Dance 16

After the dance, they form a tableau in the background

Mauxalinda enters from the mouth of the cave, followed by a servile Vendetta

They move down centre

Mauxalinda (*annoyed*) By Queen Mab's crown, despite my pow'rs,
For now, it seems, I'm beaten.
The dragon's dined too well on toast
And wildly over-eaten.
With stomach full, and sleepy eyes
He's not in any mood
For munching on a mortal maid.
He's lost the need for food.
(*Grimly*) But never fear. For when at dawn

He wakens from his sleep.
Sweet Lady Joan shall breakfast be...
She'll keep. (*Muttering*) She'll keep. She'll keep.
Vendetta Shall I chain her to the wall, Mistress?
Mauxalinda (*dismissively*) No need. For her, there's no escape.
My spells will hold her tight.
From this enchanted spot, she'll find
No path to aid her flight.
(*Firmly*) But come. There's further work to do
Before this day has passed.
And mighty Mauxalinda
Shall revenge herself at last.

She exits down L, followed by Vendetta

The creatures exit upper L and R

As they do so, Joan enters from the cave and moves down centre

Lady Joan (*glancing around fearfully*) I wish I could escape from this horrible
place, but according to Mauxalinda, all the paths lead nowhere but back here.
(*Despairing*) Oh, why did Sir Walter upset her so much? If it hadn't been for
him, Wantley would be as safe and beautiful as ever. Now it'll be destroyed
and everyone in it eaten by the dragon. Their only chance is that someone
can kill it, before it's too late. (*Sadly*) Though how can that happen if no-one
knows where it's hiding? (*Sighing*) And all I can hope is that somewhere out
there, Benjamin's still looking for me.

Song 17

At the end of the song, she sinks to her knees, crying

*A moment later, Radish's head peers round the edge of the masking flat R,
sees her, and trots down to gently nudge her*

(*Jumping to her feet; delightedly*) Radish. What are you doing here?

Radish whispers to her

You've come to rescue me? Oh, thank you Radish. (*Hugging him*) But
where's Squire Benjamin?

Radish whispers

(*Puzzled*) Climbing a rowan tree to pick berries? Whatever for? (*Hastily*) No, no. It doesn't matter. I'm sure he's got a very good reason. (*Anxiously*) But we've got to move away from here. The dragon's asleep, but he may wake up at any moment. Come on. We'll hide behind those rocks.

Joan and Radish hurry off UL

As they do so, Granny enters DR, exhausted

Granny Gubbins (*gasping*) Ooooh, I say. I've never run so fast in all my life. Fancy being chased by a ghost. It's given me a right pain in the side. (*Rubbing her side*) It was hurting so much a few minutes ago, I called the doctor on my mobile. "Oooh," he said, "A pain in the side. Do you have trouble passing water?" "No," I said, " But I sometimes feel dizzy crossing a bridge."

Jingo enters R, looking rather dishevelled

Jingo (*painfully*) Hi ya, kids.

Audience respond

Granny Gubbins (*hurrying to him; alarmed*) What happened to you?
Jingo (*wincing*) You see that ditch over there? (*He indates off R*)
Granny Gubbins (*looking off*) Yes.
Jingo (*grimacing*) Well I didn't. And now you'll have to help me look for the fifty p that dropped out of my pocket.
Granny Gubbins (*airily*) Well that won't take long. Fifty p doesn't go far these days. (*Puzzled*) But what are you doing here?
Jingo Trying to catch up with you. It'll be dark soon, and you don't want to be out here on your own, do you? Not while the dragon's still alive.
Granny Gubbins (*remembering*) You're right. We'd better start fishing.
Jingo (*puzzled*) Eh?
Granny Gubbins If ever you get lost, dig up a worm, tie it on the end of your shoelace and start fishing.
Jingo How's that going to help?
Granny Gubbins (*patiently*) Two minutes later, some idiot'll tap you on the shoulder and ask if you've got a licence.

Madge enters L with Rags and Tatters

Madge (*relieved*) Oh, thank goodness we've found you. We've been looking all over.
Rags We've just heard the weather forecast, and there's going to be a storm.
Tatters Thunder and lightning, and gallons and gallons of rain. We've got to

get back to Wantley before it starts.

Granny Gubbins (*firmly*) Not till Squire Benjamin's got his deeds back. We find him first, and then we'll go back.

Jingo (*protesting*) But we're going to get soaked.

Granny Gubbins No, we're not. We'll wait in that cave over there (*indicating the cave*) and the minute the rain stops, we can start looking again.

Madge But how do we find him?

Granny Gubbins He'll be fighting the dragon, won't he? So all we have to do is find that and he'll be there.

Jingo (*brightening*) She's right. Of course he will.

Granny Gubbins Now let's get into that cave.

She leads the way into the cave and exits. The rest follow in a line

Jingo (*in a sing-song voice*) We'll have to find the dragon.

He exits into the cave

Others (*in the same tone*) Have to find the dragon.

They exit into the cave and their voices are heard off, fading away

(*Off*) Have to find the dragon. Have to find the dragon.

They suddenly rush out again in a panic, crossing to R and huddling together

All (*gabbling*) We've found the dragon. We've found the dragon.

There is a great roar from inside the cave and a cloud of smoke issues from it. All quake and cling together

Sir Walter enters DR, his robes clutched tightly to him

Sir Walter (*scowling*) Curses. It's started to rain and I'm getting wet. I'd better take shelter at once. (*He crosses to the cave entrance*)

All (*calling urgently*) Wait. Wait.

Sir Walter (*turning to see them*) Bah. It's those stupid peasants from the village. Well if they think they're sharing my shelter, they've another think coming.

Jingo (*calling*) You can't go in there, Sir Walter.

Sir Walter (*snarling*) Nonsense. As Sir Walter of Wantley, I can do what I like. And if any of you sets foot inside this cave, you'll wish you'd never been born.

He exits into the cave

All (*cowering*) One-two-three...

The dragon roars again and smoke pours out of the cave

> *There is a shriek from Sir Walter and a moment later he comes staggering out, his clothing blackened and scorched*

Sir Walter (*weakly*) Help. Help. Save me. (*He totters* R *and collapses into their arms*)

> *There is another great bellow from the dragon, and Squire Benjamin appears* DR, *sword in hand*

Squire Benjamin (*to the others*) Stand back. (*He hurries to cave and shouts*) Come out, Master Dragon. Come face the sword of Benjamin Moore.

The dragon roars again

> (*Bravely*) You'll have to do better than that, I'm afraid. Or are your teeth only sharp enough to chew toast and marmalade?

> *Vendetta appears* UR, *seeing Squire Benjamin. He draws his own sword and creeps down behind him, ready to strike*

> (*Unaware*) Afraid to face me, are you? I thought you'd be a coward.

Vendetta prepares to strike

> *Suddenly Radish appears* UL, *and charges down to knock Vendetta to the ground*

At once, the others disarm him and take him prisoner

Squire Benjamin turns and sees this in surprise, then turns back to the cave

> Then if you won't come to me, I'd better come to you.

He enters the cave. There is a bellow from the dragon, and a cloud of smoke. Thunder and lightning begin as Squire Benjamin backs out of the cave, fighting furiously, the roars coming loud and often

Joan hurries out of hiding and joins the others

All shout encouragement as Squire Benjamin advances into the cave again, still fighting

There is more loud roaring and sound of battle, then a sudden silence. The thunder and lightning fade away and all look at the cave in concern

   Squire Benjamin emerges wearily

Squire Benjamin It's dead.

All but Vendetta cheer

Joan runs to Squire Benjamin and they embrace

Granny Gubbins (*to the audience*) Doesn't it make you want to cry? I love soppy endings.

Jingo (*brightly*) You can't leave Wantley now, Squire Benjamin. You're an absolute hero.

Madge (*happily*) Yes. And with the reward for killing the dragon, you can pay the council tax you owe and move into Moore Hall again.

   There is a flash, and Mauxalinda enters DL

Mauxalinda (*harshly*) Not so.

All recoil

> My anger knows no bounds.
> You'll ne'er possess that house and grounds.
> For though my mighty dragon's slain
> Despite your hopes, I still remain.
> (*Advancing on them*) From plagues and famine,
>   and far worse,
> You'll suffer under my new curse,
> And reel in horror when you're sent
> Another Labour government.
> (*Smirking*) Revenge indeed on those unwary
> Mortals who'd offend a fairy.

   Mother Shipton enters DR

   Chorus enter L *and* R *and form a backing*

Mother Shipton Hold fast, great Mauxalinda. Wait.
                Important news I must relate.

Mauxalinda glares at her

The Wantley forest shall not fall.
There'll be no devastation.
The county planning officers
Turned down the application.
By their decree, no trees shall face
Contractor's axe or saw,
But stay protected common land
For now and evermore.

Everyone but Sir Walter is delighted

Lady Joan (*delightedly*) Then everything's back to normal. There's nothing
to worry about.
Mauxalinda (*softening*) If that is so, I'll make it plain.
                    You'll never hear from me again.
                    I only wanted solitude.
                    Forgive me for my vengeful mood.
Mother Shipton (*brightly*) Then off to Wantley we'll away...
                    To celebrate a wedding day.
                    For now that fearsome dragon's dead,
                    Squire Benjamin and Lady Joan shall wed.
Granny Gubbins But what about him? (*Indicating Vendetta*) We don't want
him spoiling the wedding photos.
Jingo (*scowling*) I think we should kill him. (*To audience*) Don't you,
kids?

Vendetta cowers as the audience respond

Rags (*gleefully*) Let's boil him in oil.
Tatters Or make him watch (*poor quality television programme*).
Mauxalinda Wait. Wait. His faults were really mine.
                    He's stupid, coarse and bold,
                    But in defence of him I'll state
                    He only did as he was told.
Madge (*hopefully*) In that case, he could always marry me. I'd soon straighten
him out.
Vendetta (*horrified*) What? (*To Mauxalinda*) Mercy, Mistress. Mercy.

Madge grabs him and gives him a passionate kiss. All laugh

Squire Benjamin   (*stepping forward with Joan*) Then all ends well. I
                    hereby vow
                    The best of times is here and now.

Our lives we'll fill with song and laughter
And all live happily ever after.

Song 18

Lights fade rapidly at the end of the song

SCENE 6

A Corridor in Moore Hall

Jingo enters

Jingo (*calling*) Hi ya, kids.

Audience respond

Have you enjoyed yourselves?

Audience respond

Why? What have you been doing? (*Laughing*) Ooooh, you want to see the panic going on behind this curtain. They're giving Moore Hall the biggest spring-clean it's had in years. And what a wedding it's going to be. Really, really posh. They're not having finger bowls at this one, you know. After the meal's finished, we're all having showers. Mind you—we did have one little scare. When I went to collect Squire Benjamin's reward for killing the dragon, they told me there'd been a robbery at (*local High street bank*) and six masked men had stolen all the money and driven off in a getaway car they'd parked outside. (*Scornfully*) I didn't believe a word of it, though. Where could they park a getaway car in that street? Anyway, the reason I've come out here is this. I'm going to be in charge of the village choir, but everybody's rushed off to buy new clothes and things, so there's nobody left to do the practice. So I thought you could help me out. (*Beaming*) Will you do that? (*Audience response*) I've got a smashing song to practise with. It's called "I know that you must be an angel, 'cos your face looks like nothing on earth" and I'm going to sing it first, so you'll all know what it sounds like, then you can join in for the second time. All right? And don't worry about the words... I've got 'em all written down on a big board so you won't have to remember them.

Song 19

Song sheet routine is conducted as preferred and continues until the scene behind is ready

> *As the audience reaches the final line of the song, Jingo waves "cheerio" and exits, leaving them to finish*

There is a Black-out and the CURTAIN *opens onto next scene*

SCENE 7

The Banqueting Hall and Finale

Music 20

As the scene is revealed, bright music heralds the finale walk-down which is in the following order: Villagers (singers), Villagers (dancers), the Dragon (if used), Radish, Madge and Vendetta, Mother Shipton and Mauxalinda, Sir Walter, Rags and Tatters, Granny Gubbins, Jingo, Squire Benjamin and Lady Joan

When all have taken their bows, Squire Benjamin begins the final couplets

Squire Benjamin	Our pantomime is ended.
Lady Joan	This ancient tale's been told.
Mauxalinda	I've seen the error of my ways.
Mother Shipton	And now she's good as gold.
Rags	Sir Walter's had his fingers burned

Sir Walter scowls

Tatters	And Madge has got her man.

Madge beams. Vendetta winces

Granny Gubbins	But best of all it's Wedding Bells,
	For Jingo and old Gran.
Jingo	So now it time to say farewell.
	Raise high a well earned flagon.
	To those who've told the story of
All	Old Wantley and its Dragon.

There is a reprise of the finale song before the final CURTAIN *falls*

FURNITURE AND PROPERTY LIST

PROLOGUE

On stage: A gloomy grotto

ACT I

Scene 1

Set :   A medieval village setting

Off stage: A small casket (**Vendetta**)
                A bucket or watering can big enough to wear on his head (**Jingo**)

Personal: **Vendetta**: a dagger
                Mother Shipton: gnarled stick

Scene 2

Off stage: A rose with long stalk (**Mother Shipton**)

Scene 3

Set: Wantley Fayre

Scene 4

Set: Backdrop of fields and a forest

Off stage: A shopping basket covered by a soft cloth (**Madge**)

Personal: **Madge**: a five pound note
                Vendetta: a five pound note

Scene 5

Set: The Ballroom of Humbug Hall

Off stage: A sword (**Squire Benjamin**)

ACT II

SCENE 1

On stage: The village square

Off stage: Flags, balloons, flower garlands etc. (**Villagers**)

Personal: **Madge**: a five pound note
               Jingo: two five pound notes
               Sir Walter: two five pound notes

SCENE 2

Set: A path through the woods

Strike: Village square with decorations

Off stage: A sword (**Squire Benjamin**)

SCENE 3

Set: The Mayor's Parlour

Off stage: Sheets, brushes, silverware and feather dusters (**Maids and Footmen**)
               A white scroll tied with pink ribbon (**Madge**)
               A long, solid table. *On it*: a large book, rolls of wallpaper and two large sheets (**Rags and Tatters**)
               Two plastic buckets. *In each bucket*: paste and brushes. (**Rags**)
               Two plastic buckets. *In one bucket*: red emulsion paint and brush. *In the other bucket*: confetti sized scraps of mixed coloured paper and tin-foil, or polystyrene beads. (**Tatters**)
               A tall step-ladder (**Tatters**)

SCENE 4

Set: A rocky gorge

SCENE 5

Set: Outside the dragon's lair

Off stage: A sword (**Squire Benjamin**)

SCENE 6

Set: A corridor in Moore Hall

SCENE 7

Set: A banqueting hall

LIGHTING PLOT

PROLOGUE

To open : Red and green light on **Mauxalinda**

Cue 1	**Mauxalinda** laughs and exits *Lights go out*	(Page 1)

ACT I, SCENE 1

To open : General bright, sunny, exterior lighting

Cue 2	**Lady Joan** and **Granny Gubbins** exit UR *Lights dim*	(Page 8)
Cue 3	**Mauxalinda** enters DL *Green light on* **Mauxalinda**	(Page 8)
Cue 4	**Vendetta** hurries after **Mauxalinda** *Green light fades, return to sunny, exterior lighting*	(Page 9)
Cue 5	At end of scene *Rapid fade*	(Page 18)

ACT I, SCENE 2

To open : General bright, sunny, exterior lighting

Cue 6	**Sir Walter** rushes off R chased by **Vendetta** *Rapid fade*	(Page 23)

ACT I, SCENE 3

To open : General effect of bright, sunny day

Cue 7	**Mauxalinda** appears L *Green follow-spot on* **Mauxalinda**	(Page 26)
Cue 8	**Mauxalinda** exits L *Green follow-spot goes out*	(Page 27)

Cue 9   At end of scene   (Page 30)
                 Rapid fade

ACT I, SCENE 4

To open : General bright, sunny, exterior lighting

Cue 10   **Rags** exits R, followed by **Tatters**   (Page 33)
                 Fade to Black-out

ACT I, SCENE 5

To open : General interior lighting

Cue 11   **Mauxalinda** enters DL   (Page 38)
                 Green light on **Mauxalinda**

Cue 12   **Mauxalinda** exits L   (Page 39)
                 Green light goes out

Cue 13   At end of the song   (Page 40)
                 Lights fade to Black-out

ACT II, SCENE 1

To open : General exterior lighting

Cue 14   At end of the song   (Page 47)
                 Rapid fade

ACT II, SCENE 2

To open : Subdued lighting

Cue 15   At end of the song   (Page 50)
                 Rapid fade

ACT II, SCENE 3

To open : General interior lighting

Cue 16   **Jingo** hurls contents into the audience   (Page 58)
                 Instant Black-out

ACT II, SCENE 4

To open : After a roar, the lights slowly come up to semi-darkness

Lighting Plot   79

EFFECTS PLOT

ACT I

ACT II

Cue 12   **Squire Benjamin** enters the cave a second time   (Page 69)
             The roars stop suddenly, thunder and lightning fade

Cue 13   **Madge**: "...Moore Hall again."   (Page 70)
             A flash